Christian Morning Motivation

STRENGTHEN YOUR DAY WITH 98 DAILY DEVOTIONALS FUELED BY GOD'S WORD

AMY HUNTER

HEALTHY HAPPY FARM

To:

_____

_____

_____

from:

_____

_____

In Loving Memory of
Amanda,

You inspired and motivated me to keep
writing and working on this project. I'm
deeply sorry I couldn't share this book
with you in time. I pray that your
memory will forever bring hope, healing,
and understanding to those in need. Your
presence is greatly missed, but I know
you are in good hands.

Love you always,

Contents

"But we all, with unveiled face seeing the glory of the Lord as in a mirror, are transformed into the same image from glory to glory, even as from the Lord, the Spirit." 2 Corinthians 3:18

Intro

"BUT WE ALL, WITH UNVEILED FACE SEEING THE GLORY OF THE LORD AS IN A MIRROR, ARE TRANSFORMED INTO THE SAME IMAGE FROM GLORY TO GLORY, EVEN AS FROM THE LORD, THE SPIRIT." 2 CORINTHIANS 3:18

Dear Reader,

I am incredibly grateful that you've chosen to pick up this morning devotional. The opportunity to accompany you on this transformative journey, where we place God at the center of everything, fills me with joy. I invite you to challenge yourself to prioritize scripture reading at the start of each day.

Anchoring yourself to God's Word will empower you to navigate whatever the day presents.

Over the upcoming 14 weeks, we'll delve into 7 distinct topics, dedicating two weeks to each one. This extended period will allow for thoughtful contemplation and meaningful growth. I am genuinely thrilled to join you on this path, confident that together, we can establish a daily routine of prioritizing God and working towards aligning our minds with the teachings of Christ.

Feel free to connect with the Scriptures in the translation that resonates most with you. In this book, I've opted for the World English Bible (WEB) translation due to its lack of copyright restrictions.

My intention is for this book to become a practical and inspiring resource for you. While I do not claim to be an authority figure or a professional, my love for God and the positive impact He's had on my life compel me to assist others on their journeys. Consider this book a friendly and uplifting guide rather than an instructional manual. Should my perspective on scripture differ from yours, I encourage you to rely solely on the Bible as the ultimate authority, as I, too, am learning alongside you.

My prayer is that as we prioritize seeking God each day, He will work within us, gradually transforming our hearts and attitudes, and illuminating our lives with His glory, one step at a time.

On a side note, I would greatly appreciate it if you could share your thoughts and feedback by leaving a review of the book on the platform of your purchase. Your review not only aids me but also assists others in determining if this book suits them. Your input can truly make a significant impact!

Once again, I extend my heartfelt gratitude for investing in this book. I eagerly anticipate embarking on this journey together. Remember, sharing devotionals with a friend or loved one can enhance the experience. If you know someone who might benefit from a copy, please do not hesitate to share it with them.

With Love,

Amy

Choosing Joy

Breaking Free from Negativity

"Don't be fashioned according to this world, but be transformed by the renewing of your mind, so that you may prove what is the good and acceptable and perfect will of God." Romans 12:2

Good morning!

Today is a new day and an opportunity for a fresh start. In Romans 12:2, we are encouraged not to conform to the ways of the world but to be transformed by the renewing of our minds. This is an ongoing process, and each day allows us to move closer to God's perfect will.

When you **HOPE** this morning, how did you feel?
Were you **1 PETER 1:3** the day ahead and ready to
get it over **HOPE** ore it even started? If so, avoid
setting yo **1 PETER 1:3** for failure with these thoughts.
Our thoug **1 PETER 1:3** a powerful impact on how we
perceive situations and others. By intentionally
building a new routine and training ourselves to
seek a more positive thought process, we can renew
our minds and learn how to inspire, strengthen, and
encourage others.

Remember that each day is a new opportunity to
grow and live in a way that honors God. Let's trust in
His guidance and approach this day with positivity
and hope.

Smile because it's going to be a great day!

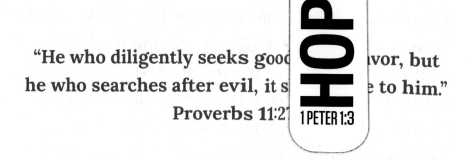

"He who diligently seeks good [...] vor, but he who searches after evil, it s[...] e to him."
Proverbs 11:2[...]

Good morning!

As I woke up this morning, my heart was filled with a prayer for my family to see the inherent goodness in others. Every person has a seed of goodness in their heart waiting to be nurtured.

Reflecting on past conversations, I recalled a time when someone asked, "What about the really bad people?" This question brought to light a fundamental truth that we do not and cannot know what's in others' hearts. However, we do know that God calls us to be kind even to our enemies.

In 2 Timothy 2:23-26, it says, "The Lord's servant must not quarrel, but be gentle toward all, able to teach, patient, in gentleness correcting those who oppose him: perhaps God may give them repentance leading to a full knowledge of the truth,

When you woke up this morning, how did you feel? Were you dreading the day ahead and ready to get it over with before it even started? If so, avoid setting yourself up for failure with these thoughts. Our thoughts have a powerful impact on how we perceive situations and others. By intentionally building a new routine and training ourselves to seek a more positive thought process, we can renew our minds and learn how to inspire, strengthen, and encourage others.

Remember that each day is a new opportunity to grow and live in a way that honors God. Let's trust in His guidance and approach this day with positivity and hope.

Smile because it's going to be a great day!

"He who diligently seeks good seeks favor, but he who searches after evil, it shall come to him."
Proverbs 11:27

Good morning!

As I woke up this morning, my heart was filled with a prayer for my family to see the inherent goodness in others. Every person has a seed of goodness in their heart waiting to be nurtured.

Reflecting on past conversations, I recalled a time when someone asked, "What about the really bad people?" This question brought to light a fundamental truth that we do not and cannot know what's in others' hearts. However, we do know that God calls us to be kind even to our enemies.

In 2 Timothy 2:23-26, it says, "The Lord's servant must not quarrel, but be gentle toward all, able to teach, patient, in gentleness correcting those who oppose him: perhaps God may give them repentance leading to a full knowledge of the truth, and they may recover themselves out of the devil's snare, having been taken captive by him to his will."

It's important to remember that it's not our job to judge who is good or bad. We can never truly see what is in a person's heart or what has led them to where they are. Our perspective on life can be influenced by what we choose to look for or expect to see. If we constantly search for mistakes and faults in others, we will surely find them. However, if we look for the goodness and beauty that God has placed within each person, we will find it.

To change the direction of our thoughts, we need to be intentional about catching ourselves when we have negative thoughts about others. Instead of labeling someone as annoying or difficult, we can ask ourselves, "Is that true? How do I know? Could this person be going through a tough time?" Let's make a conscious effort to let go of negative thoughts and attempt to show kindness in every circumstance.

Have a great day!

"A cheerful heart makes good medicine, but a crushed spirit dries up the bones." Proverbs 17:22

Good morning!

Can we choose to be cheerful? When we have a list of things that need to be done, bills that need to be paid, and errands we would rather skip, it can feel overwhelming. It's an unavoidable list that can bring us down, so how can we be cheerful about it?

One way to do this is to write down our to-do list, giving us a clear action plan. Once we have a plan, we don't need to keep thinking about it and weighing ourselves down with unnecessary worry. Instead, we can focus on our goals and accomplishments, checking off each task as we complete it. It's a small but effective way to boost our mood and stay motivated.

Jesus is an excellent example of someone who walked on this earth with a cheerful heart despite facing many difficult challenges. He taught us that through prayer and faith, we can tackle hard things and remain positive. Imagine how different the world would be if Jesus had gone around with a crushed spirit, reminding everyone of His struggles.

So if you're feeling overwhelmed today, take a deep breath, write your list down, and pray about it. Don't let anything crush your spirit or steal your joy. You have the power to be like good medicine for those around you. You never know who might desperately need your smile today.

Let's choose to have a cheerful heart today, and may it bring light to those around us.

Have a great day!

"You are the light of the world. A city located on a hill can't be hidden. Neither do you light a lamp, and put it under a measuring basket, but on a stand, and it shines to all who are in the house. Even so, let your light shine before men; that they may see your good works, and glorify your Father who is in heaven." Matthew 5:14-16

Good morning!

Many of us feel uncomfortable being in the spotlight, myself included. Even simple conversations can leave us at a loss for words, and public speaking is a challenge. We worry about forgetting our lines, stumbling over our words, and fidgeting nervously. But the truth is, whether we realize it or not, we are always in the spotlight. Our words, actions, and attitudes are noticed by those around us, and we have the opportunity to be a positive influence.

As Christians, we are called to be a light in the world and to stand out by being examples of love, kindness, and generosity. Think of the people you know who positively stand out. What qualities do they possess? How do they make you feel when you're around them?

Even in difficult situations, we can choose to be a light. When dealing with a difficult person or circumstance, let's challenge ourselves to respond with kindness and grace. Let's strive to glorify God in everything we do, knowing that our actions can have a powerful impact on those around us.

So let's embrace the spotlight, knowing that our words and actions matter. Let's be intentional about being a positive influence, and trust that God will use us to make a difference in the world.

Have a great day!

"This is the day that Yahweh has made. We will rejoice and be glad in it!" Psalms 118:24

Good morning!

I often speak about my desire for happiness, and sometimes I even imagine that certain possessions or achievements will bring me joy. However, as followers of Jesus, we don't need to search for happiness because we can be satisfied with the joy that comes from knowing God cares for us and that our lives are in His hands.

While happiness is often a choice, it's only a temporary emotion. It's unrealistic to think that we can experience just one emotion throughout our lives. Achieving our goals may make us feel great for a while, but then what? Does getting a car, job, or puppy suddenly make us happier?

The dopamine produced while hoping and waiting for something to make us happy can become addictive. Once we achieve one goal, we may develop another, and then another, and then we can end up in a never-ending cycle of always wanting something new to feel happy, never finding contentment until we reach our next goal. So how do we break this cycle?

Today, if you're searching for happiness, focus on the blessings in your life. Be grateful, joyful, and content with where you are right now. If you're going through a tough time, be glad that it won't last forever. Remember that God hears your prayers and will never abandon you.

Have a great day!

"I have spoken these things to you, that my joy may remain in you, and that your joy may be made full."
John 15:11

Good morning!

Jesus wants His joy to remain in us. Let that sink in for a moment. He desires for us to be joyful people, not hardened by the world, bitter, envious, or broken inside. Jesus gives us the strength to be joyful even in a chaotic world.

We must be mindful of negative thoughts that creep into our minds. Where do they come from, and can we stop them? We can make a conscious effort to halt our thoughts in their tracks. For example, when we see someone driving in a car that we wish we had, we must stop that train of thought rather than entertain it, which will lead to jealousy and frustration.

If we see someone being rude and start to judge them, we must stop right there and move on to what we're supposed to be doing. We can set an example for someone with good morals. Similarly, if someone doesn't clean up after themselves and we get angry or contemplate leaving a mess for them, we must stop those kinds of irrational thoughts from persisting.

If we stop listening to our negative thoughts and choose to re-focus on what Jesus asks us to do, we can be filled with His joy. We can find joy even in the midst of chaos because Jesus gives us the strength to persevere.

Dear God, please help us to focus our attention on what is good so that we may experience your joy throughout our day. Amen.

Have a great day!

"You have turned my mourning into dancing for me. You have removed my sackcloth, and clothed me with gladness," Psalms 30:11

Good morning!

Have you ever felt guilty about something you did or felt sorrowful and grieved? It can be tough to have a sleepless night filled with tossing, turning, thinking, praying, crying, and waking up feeling like you were hit by a truck. If you feel that way today, I'm sorry you're hurting, but remember that God hears and knows everything you're going through, even if you can't see His plan.

This verse talks about wearing a sackcloth which was made of thick and scratchy material similar to that found on a potato sack. People would wear it when feeling sorry or grieving until they decided to let go of their sorrow and trust God.

Can you imagine taking off a sackcloth? It was a symbol of letting go of your pain, and not only would you feel better, but everyone else would see it too.

God can comfort you and give you gladness again. Today is a new day, and you don't have to hold onto your feelings of guilt or grief. Take off your sackcloth and face the day ahead. And if you're not in this situation, I encourage you to smile and offer comfort to others. You never know what they might be going through today.

Have a great day!

"that they do good, that they be rich in good works, that they be ready to distribute, willing to communicate;" 1 Timothy 6:18

Good morning!

I woke up today with a strong desire to help others, as I often do. This has been my passion since childhood. When I was young, I wanted to be a doctor so that I could save lives. Later, I wanted to be a physical therapist to help people strengthen their bodies, and then I decided I would like to be a counselor to lend an ear to those in need. Today, I work as a cashier.

Although it may not seem like much to some people, my job is important. I greet customers with a smile and wish them a great day when they leave. I am a familiar face to many, and while I may need to work on my communication skills, I am always willing to have a friendly conversation.

Sometimes, my coworkers feel like our job isn't something to be proud of, but every job that contributes to the greater good is essential. Don't let self-doubt or the opinions of others make you feel less valuable because of your position.

Remember, you are a child of God, and it is your duty to do good. That's it! It doesn't matter if you're a stay-at-home parent, a software developer, a police officer, or a custodian. We can all communicate with kindness and show compassion. Today, let's spread positivity and communicate in an uplifting way.

Have a great day!

"whom, not having known, you love. In him, though now you don't see him, yet believing, you rejoice greatly with joy that is unspeakable and full of glory" 1 Peter 1:8

Good morning!

The Bible truly is an amazing book. Learning about its history and seeing pictures of the ancient text is fascinating. It is awe-inspiring to see how God has spoken to people throughout history, revealing the truth of His word.

During Jesus' time on earth, many people were able to witness His miracles and hear His teachings in person. They had a unique opportunity to love and worship Him.

However, there were many more people during that time who didn't have the chance to see Jesus in person, yet they still believed and rejoiced in the good news. They experienced the joy that comes from knowing Jesus, even without seeing him face to face. We can relate to that today, can't we?

God makes His word known to us exactly when we need to hear it. There is no greater reason to be filled with joy than knowing and believing in Jesus. So let's rejoice today with the uncontainable joy that comes from having a relationship with him.

Have a great day!

"throwing down imaginations and every high thing that is exalted against the knowledge of God, and bringing every thought into captivity to the obedience of Christ;" 2 Corinthians 10:5

Good morning!

Have you ever heard the phrase "think before you speak"? Well, have you ever considered the idea of "thinking before you think"? I've realized that I tend to focus on the negatives of situations before the positives, and it's a habit I want to break. When I don't intentionally choose to think kind and godly thoughts, I find myself seeing problems everywhere and judging everyone I meet.

For example, if I greet someone and they don't respond, my initial thoughts might be, "That was rude" or "Do they have a problem with me?" Instead of considering other possibilities, such as maybe they didn't hear me, or they're preoccupied with something else, I'm assuming the worst and creating negative scenarios in my mind.

However, we can never truly know what someone else is going through or thinking. Even if they're intentionally doing something hurtful, God calls us to forgive and love them anyway. If we don't learn to forgive and love others, we're not obeying Christ.

Another way we can create negative scenarios is by judging others based on their appearance. For instance, if someone looks wealthy, I might assume that their life is easier. Conversely, if someone looks rough, I might imagine that they've made poor life choices. But who am I to create stories about other people's lives? Only God knows their struggles and how they've achieved their success.

Today, let's be mindful of our thoughts and refocus them on what is true and good. By intentionally choosing kind and godly thoughts, we can break the cycle of negativity and bring more positivity into our lives.

Have a great day!

"But the fruit of the Spirit is love, joy, peace, patience, kindness, goodness, faith, gentleness, and self-control. Against such things there is no law." Galatians 5:22-23

Good morning!

Yesterday, I woke up intending to have a great day with my kids. However, while they were playing with their toys, I tried to work on my writing, which ended up in frustration when my five-year-old's toy started dancing on my work, and my two-year-old demanded my attention. Despite my attempts to get them to play with their toys instead, I kept losing the battle and eventually snapped at them, pushing them away.

Later on, I realized my mistake - I had lost sight of my original goal, which was to have a great day with my kids. If I had focused on that, I would have watched and played with them rather than attempting to get some work done. I failed to show them love, joy, peace, patience, kindness, goodness, faith, gentleness, and self-control, which would have led to a much better outcome.

Today, I will try to shift my thinking to what I can do with my kids rather than what I can't accomplish. Instead of getting frustrated by my limitations, I will celebrate the little achievements we make together throughout the day. By doing so, we can have a better day and perhaps accomplish a few chores as well.

Remember that the fruit of the Spirit is love, joy, peace, patience, kindness, goodness, faith, gentleness, and self-control. Let's not forget to recognize our blessings and show these loving qualities in all that we do.

What do you struggle with? Can you use self-control to shift your thoughts more positively?

Have a great day!

"Sing, heavens; and be joyful, earth; and break out into singing, mountains: for Yahweh has comforted his people, and will have compassion on his afflicted." Isaiah 49:13

Good morning!

Are you feeling ready to take on the day? I sure am! As a morning person, I can't help but feel a little extra cheerful, especially after reading a verse that speaks to the joy and grace that God offers us. It's a great reason to smile, sing, and be glad as we go about our day.

But why aren't more people walking around with a pep in their step and a smile on their face? I think people unknowingly let the obstacles in their lives become the faces they wear. When you wake up, what are your first thoughts? Do you start your day by thanking God for all He's done and asking for guidance, or are your first thoughts about your sore neck from that awkward pillow, the lack of sleep you had, and how you somehow already know it's going to be a long day?

Our first thoughts can set the tone for the day. If we pay attention to what we are thinking, we can redirect our thoughts to where they should be. When we make an effort to refocus our thoughts on God, our frustrations and worries will not seem so bad.

If you had a tough night, be happy that it's a new day full of new opportunities! Let's choose to get up singing with hope and trust. I pray that the tune of your day is a happy one.

Have a great day!

"I know that there is nothing better for them than to rejoice, and to do good as long as they live. Also that every man should eat and drink, and enjoy good in all his labor, is the gift of God." Ecclesiastes 3:12-13

Good morning!

There's something so special about starting a new day with a positive mindset. I usually wake up with a sense of excitement and enthusiasm for what's to come. However, by the afternoon, my enthusiasm slows down quite a bit. Just when it seems like the rest of the world is waking up, I start to feel my energy dwindling and my patience wearing thin.

If I find myself struggling to maintain my positive attitude, I need to take a moment to reflect on what might be contributing to my feelings. Sometimes, I just need a quick snack or a brief walk to refocus my energy. Regardless of the cause, I know that it's important for me to take control of my attitude and make sure it's not affecting those around me negatively.

As Christians, we are ambassadors of Christ, it's essential to remember that others are watching how we respond and react to life's challenges. We have an opportunity to reflect Jesus in our lives and to show others who He is through our actions. While none of us are perfect, we can still strive to be the best versions of ourselves and to make a positive impact on those around us.

So today, I encourage you to rejoice, do good, and embrace the joy and blessings that God has given you.

Have a great Day!

"Rejoice always. Pray without ceasing. In everything give thanks, for this is the will of God in Christ Jesus toward you." 1 Thessalonians 5:16-18

Good morning!

The word "rejoice" often evokes images of joyous celebration, such as the singing of angels at the birth of Christ or the beauty of a sunrise. However, the call to "rejoice always" can be challenging, especially when things don't go according to plan.

For instance, It's easy for me to rejoice when I can enjoy a nice cup of coffee, but it's definitely a challenge to rejoice when I accidentally knock it off the table.

It can be tough to maintain a sense of joy and gratitude in the face of obstacles and difficulties, but these trials can also offer growth opportunities. Just as Jesus endured unimaginable situations and taught us to have faith, we, too, can learn from our experiences and become stronger through them.

It's also important to be thankful for the blessings we do have, even when things aren't going as we had hoped. If we spilled our coffee, we could be grateful that no one got hurt and that we have the means to clean it up. We can find joy in the little things, even amidst our struggles.

Remember, God's will for us is to rejoice always, pray without ceasing, and give thanks in everything. By doing so, we can find peace and contentment in even the most difficult circumstances. If things aren't going your way today, rejoice for your growth, pray for guidance, and be thankful that you can move on.

Have a great day!

Fearless Faith

Developing Confidence and Courage Through Christ

"I will tell the north, 'Give them up!' and tell the south, 'Don't hold them back! Bring my sons from far, and my daughters from the ends of the earth— everyone who is called by my name, and whom I have created for my glory, whom I have formed, yes, whom I have made." Isaiah 43:6-7

Good morning!

As children of God and followers of Christ, we are called to glorify His name. This means that we reflect the goodness and beauty of who He is through our actions and lives. Jesus showed us the way by living a righteous life, exhibiting qualities such as kindness, compassion, and forgiveness. He also taught us how to resist the temptations of the Devil with faith and scripture.

As Christians called by His name, we have a purpose and a mission to live in a way that truly honors God. Though we are not perfect and will make mistakes, God is still at work in us, molding and shaping us into who He intended us to be.

God created us with love and care and has a magnificent plan for each and every one of us. So hold your head high, knowing that He loves you deeply and has only the best in store for you.

Have a great day!

"For him who knew no sin he made to be sin on our behalf; so that in him we might become the righteousness of God." 2 Corinthians 5:21

Good morning!

Embracing change is a journey of strength and courage. Transforming one's life, breaking away from familiar surroundings and habits, and choosing a path that aligns with the teachings of God, is a bold and commendable decision. But it is not an easy one.

In a world that often tolerates and even promotes sin, taking a stand for what is right can lead to questioning and criticism, especially from those who are not ready to change themselves. And sometimes, the most challenging part of change is overcoming the self-doubt and guilt from the past. But it is never too late to become a new person.

I speak from experience; the person I am today is a far cry from the shy and rebellious individual I once was. But even now, there are moments when the memories of my past return, and I question my worthiness of forgiveness.

Let me assure you no matter how great or small, your sins are forgiven because of the sacrifice of Jesus on the cross. He has redeemed us, and with each passing moment, we have the opportunity to become a new person in Him.

So let us be courageous in making the right choices, regardless of what others may say or do. Let's live with purpose and righteousness, uncovering a greater joy in life.

Have a great day!

"But the very hairs of your head are all counted. Therefore don't be afraid. You are of more value than many sparrows." Luke 12:7

Good morning!

Do you ever feel like you're not enough? That you're unloved, unattractive, unintelligent, or inadequate? It's natural to have these thoughts, but I want you to know that they couldn't be further from the truth. In fact, the very hairs of your head are all counted, and in the eyes of the Lord, you are precious, valued, and loved.

Maybe you've experienced hurtful words or actions from others in the past, and it's left you feeling down. But please don't base your self-worth on their opinions. People's judgments are often clouded by their own insecurities and biases, but your worth is not determined by their flawed perspectives. Only your creator truly knows you and has the right to define who you are, and He says you are worth dying for.

Remember, who you are today is not set in stone. Your past experiences, your current surroundings, and the choices you've made do not define you. You can change and grow to become the person you were always meant to be. And through it all, you can take comfort in the fact that God loves you dearly and sees your true value.

So don't be afraid, my friend. You are more valuable than many sparrows, and your potential is limitless.

Have a great day!

"If I have made gold my hope, and have said to the fine gold, 'You are my confidence;'" Job 31:24

Good morning!

Have you ever considered the idea that the grass is always greener on the other side? It's amusing how we become envious and yearn for what we see others having – be it fun experiences, luxurious trips, flashy cars, or even attractive appearances. Social media has a way of distorting our perceptions of reality, only showing us a small fraction of someone else's life. We never see the struggles they may face or the sacrifices they've made to get there. Life is not a competition, and it's important to remember that everyone's journey is unique.

I have a horse with a sprawling pasture, yet he always strains his neck toward the grass beyond the fence, as if it's the most beautiful sight he's ever seen. It's funny, yet sad, to see him focusing on something he can't have, neglecting all the greenery he already has surrounding him. Every once in a while, I let him out, and he jumps with joy to the spot he's been gazing at. He eats ravenously, tearing at the blades as fast as he can. But soon, he begins to notice the things hidden in the grass – the sticks, the toys, and even our dog's droppings – and suddenly, he's no longer content. He realizes that he has everything he needs within his own fence.

Just like my horse, our focus should not be on worldly possessions that come and go, but on the Lord who is constant and steadfast in our lives. We can have confidence in His love and guidance, knowing that He will see us through life's challenges and obstacles. If we place our trust in anything other than God, we will always be on the wrong side of the fence.

Have a great day!

"He said, "Come!" Peter stepped down from the boat, and walked on the waters to come to Jesus. But when he saw that the wind was strong, he was afraid, and beginning to sink, he cried out, saying, "Lord, save me!" Matthew 14:29-30

Good morning!

The story of Peter and Jesus walking on the water is an inspiring reminder of the power of faith. As we journey through life, it can be easy to lose sight of the things that truly matter, but like Peter, we must keep our eyes fixed on Jesus, even when the winds and waves seem to be against us.

Peter had the courage to step out of the boat and walk toward Jesus, but when he let fear take hold, he lost sight of his goal. We, too, may be faced with doubt and uncertainty, but it is important to remember that God is always with us, guiding us and helping us to keep moving forward.

When we take a step in a new direction, we may get discouraged and full of worries and doubts, but we can pray and trust that God is working in ways we can't imagine. Whether we succeed or stumble along the way, the journey is worth taking because we never know what blessings and opportunities may be waiting for us.

Have a great day!

"Such confidence we have through Christ toward God; not that we are sufficient of ourselves, to account anything as from ourselves; but our sufficiency is from God; who also made us sufficient as servants of a new covenant; not of the letter, but of the Spirit. For the letter kills, but the Spirit gives life." 2 Corinthians 3:4-6

Good morning!

Have you ever felt intimidated by tasks assigned to you, feeling like you lack the skills and qualifications to do them well? I can relate to that feeling. Sometimes when I sit down to write, doubts creep in, and I wonder if my words are worth reading. I question my abilities and feel unqualified to talk about the Bible and how it relates to our lives.

But here's the thing, I am reminded that I am not alone in this journey. With God's help and guidance through prayer and studying the scriptures, I find the confidence I need to keep going. I know that my confidence doesn't come from within myself but from the belief that God will use me to reach others and make a difference. I trust that even if my writing is a disorganized mess, God can still use it for good. With the spirit of God within me, I am made sufficient to serve Him.

If you, too, feel intimidated or nervous about a new challenge in your life, remember that you can have complete confidence in the Lord. You are qualified, worthy, and enough with Christ in your heart. He will give you the strength needed to persevere and overcome any obstacle.

Have a great day!

"Saul said to David, "You are not able to go against this Philistine to fight with him; for you are but a youth, and he a man of war from his youth." 1 Samuel 17:33

Good morning!

It's amazing to think about David, who defied all odds and faced a seemingly insurmountable challenge with unwavering faith and courage. Despite being dismissed by those around him as a mere young boy, David trusted in the Lord and believed that he had what it takes to defeat the giant warrior Goliath.

It takes true bravery to ignore the negativity and doubts of others and to follow one's own intuition, and David's unwavering faith in God's guidance is truly inspiring. He never allowed self-doubt to cloud his mind or compromise his mission, and his unwavering belief in God's power led to his ultimate triumph.

It can be all too easy to let our own fears and insecurities hold us back and to seek validation from others, but like David, we must have faith that God is always with us and guiding us. Whether you are pursuing a giant, a goal, or a dream, have the courage to chase after it with all your might and trust that with God on your side, you can do anything!

Have a great day!

"I know your works (behold, I have set before you an open door, which no one can shut), that you have a little power, and kept my word, and didn't deny my name." Revelation 3:8

Good morning!

God has the power to open doors for us that we never knew existed, leading us to amazing and unexpected places. Have you ever been surprised by a door that God has opened for you?

As a young girl, I struggled with learning how to read and write in school. English was a challenge for me in every aspect, from spelling and reading comprehension to writing and sentence structure. I never enjoyed reading books or writing papers. Yet, today, I am filled with a deep passion and drive to write. God knows my heart better than I ever could, and He has guided me to where I am now.

What if the door doesn't seem to open? If you have prayed about your dreams and asked for God's guidance, rest assured that He will not let you down.

He can see the big picture and knows what's best for us, even if our plans don't align with His. Looking back, I'm grateful that God didn't give me everything I prayed for. He answered prayers I didn't know I had, leading me to a life that was even better than I ever could have imagined.

If the door doesn't seem to budge, it may not be the right time or the right door. God promises to take care of us no matter what the situation is. Have faith and trust in His plan for your life. He has something special just for you!

Have a great day!

"Humble yourselves therefore under the mighty hand of God, that he may exalt you in due time; casting all your worries on him, because he cares for you." 1 Peter 5:6-7

Good morning!

Do you ever feel overwhelmed by the long list of tasks that you need to accomplish? This morning, I found myself weighed down by the thought of everything I had to do, to the point where I didn't even feel like getting out of bed. I realized that I was trying to tackle everything on my own without giving my worries to God.

I took a deep breath and prayed to God, asking for help and guidance. I realized that I needed to humble myself and remember that God is in control. Instead of carrying the weight of the day on my shoulders, I could give it all to God and start working for Him.

The truth is God loves us and will take care of us. If we do our best, we can trust that whatever needs to be done will be done. So, if you are worried about anything today, I encourage you to give it to God. You don't have to carry the load alone. He will provide you with the help you need.

Have a great day!

"But you are a chosen race, a royal priesthood, a holy nation, a people for God's own possession, that you may proclaim the excellence of him who called you out of darkness into his marvelous light:" 1 Peter 2:9

Good morning!

Do you feel like royalty? Some people see themselves as inferior to others and think so little of themselves because they don't understand how special they are to God. As a child, I struggled with low self-esteem. I had no problem loving and seeing the beauty in others, but I just couldn't get past my imperfections. I listened to the negative thoughts that popped into my head and hosted many pity parties. I remember praying and asking God why He made me the way He did. My insecurities and inability to see the silver lining led to years of careless and self-destructive behavior. I was lost, and I didn't know it.

I thought life was a hard, sad, and lonely place. That was until I decided to let go of my negative feelings and turn to God. I dedicated my time to reading and listening to the Bible. I searched through devotionals, attended many different churches, and prayed often. I let go of anything that brought me down, including music, movies, and friends. I found a safe place to connect with God and work toward fighting off negativity. Before I knew it, I was a whole new person inside and out.

Today, I refuse to be drawn back into the brokenness I once experienced. I love the life God gave me, and I can't wait to see how He uses it. Jesus is calling us to be His royal priesthood, and we should act like it. Treat yourself like the royalty you are. Walk with confidence in Him and care for the well-being of others by sharing the wonderful things He does in your life. You are precious to Him.

Have a great day!

"Blessed is the man who trusts in Yahweh, and whose confidence is in Yahweh. For he shall be as a tree planted by the waters, who spreads out its roots by the river, and shall not fear when heat comes, but its leaf shall be green; and shall not be careful in the year of drought, neither shall cease from yielding fruit." Jeremiah 17:7-8

Good morning!

I love the visualization of this passage. When we trust and have confidence in the Lord, we can go out into the world knowing we will be taken care of like a tree planted next to a river. Even in extreme heat or drought, we do not have to fear because we will always have access to the water He provides.

When life events happen, and we feel nervous, weak, or afraid of what will come, we can have complete confidence knowing that God will provide for us. In John 4:14, Jesus said, "But whoever drinks of the water that I will give him will never thirst again; but the water that I will give him will become in him a well of water springing up to eternal life."

Do you believe what Jesus said? If so, then you have nothing to worry about because you have everything you need to withstand the heat and the challenges coming your way. Today, if you get caught up in thoughts of uncertainty, remember that Jesus gave you a well, and you can drink from it anytime.

Have a great day!

"For God didn't give us a spirit of fear, but of power, love, and self-control." 2 Timothy 1:7

Good morning!

If God didn't give us a spirit of fear, then where does it come from? Fear of loss and failure can hold us back from trying something new or even giving up when things get tough.

I remember when my daughter was three years old, she was determined to ride a bicycle. She climbed up on her little pink bike with training wheels and tried to ride it. Her small legs could barely reach the pedals, and she didn't have enough strength to make it go. One day, after an hour or so of pushing her over and over again, I got tired and told her to get down and walk. She begged me for one more push, so I gave her an extra strong one. Meanwhile, she turned her wheel just a bit so that she could push with all her might. The bike tipped over, and she fell to the ground. She immediately lost her desire to ride a bike and gained a fear of trying it again.

Two years later, even with the training wheels on, she still has a hard time finding the courage to ride her bike. It saddens me to know that she could be enjoying a nice bike ride on a sunny summer day if she would face her fears and try again. Yes, she might fall, and she might not get it right away, but I know it would be worth the effort.

I wonder if this is a little glimpse of how God feels when we pass on something we are called to do because we are afraid of failing. Do you think God gets a little sad when we give up on our dreams or goals? Knowing how much happier we would be if we would just dust ourselves off and try again. God commands us not to fear. Don't give up so easily on your goals. It might be worth the effort.

Have a great day!

"For you formed my inmost being. You knit me together in my mother's womb. I will give thanks to you, for I am fearfully and wonderfully made. Your works are wonderful. My soul knows that very well." Psalms 139:13-14

Good morning!

This is a beautiful reminder of how thoughtfully and carefully God created each one of us. We are not just a result of chance or random circumstances, but rather, God formed our inmost being and knit us together with love and intention. This truth should bring us comfort and peace, knowing that we are fearfully and wonderfully made by a loving Creator.

It's understandable to question why God would create us with imperfections or difficulties, but it's important to remember that these experiences can shape us and help us grow. They can teach us valuable lessons, develop our character, and increase our compassion for others. And in the end, they can bring us closer to God as we seek his comfort, guidance, and strength.

So today, embrace the unique person that God has created you to be. Celebrate your strengths and work through your weaknesses, knowing that God is with you every step of the way. You are valuable, loved, and have a purpose in this world.

Have a great day!

"The Spirit himself testifies with our spirit that we are children of God; and if children, then heirs; heirs of God, and joint heirs with Christ; if indeed we suffer with him, that we may also be glorified with him." Romans 8:16-17

Good morning!

Who are you? If you believe that Jesus is the Son of God who died and rose again, then you are a child of God and an heir to his kingdom with Jesus. What does that mean to you?

To me, it means that Jesus' suffering and sacrifice for us resulted in the forgiveness of our sins. He not only paid for our sins but also granted us access to the kingdom of God. Through the Holy Spirit, we can suffer, rejoice, and be glorified with Him in heaven. Take a moment to read John 14, where Jesus explains that He will prepare a place for us and send the Spirit of truth to live in us. What a wonderful God we serve!

Why am I saying this? I want to emphasize how special you are. God loves you so much that he sent His son to live and die for you. When your time on earth is over, you will be sent to live with God and His glory. Never doubt your worth. The enemy may try to deceive and tempt you, but you must hold your head up and walk in righteousness because you are a child of God!

Have a great day!

Love in Action

CULTIVATING COMPASSION AND CONNECTION THROUGH GOD'S LOVE

"If a man says, 'I love God,' and hates his brother, he is a liar; for he who doesn't love his brother whom he has seen, how can he love God whom he has not seen?" 1 John 4:20

Good morning!

Isn't that verse a simple but profound truth? It requires us to examine our hearts and get rid of any negative feelings we have toward others. Although people can be cruel and are capable of terrible acts, we also have the potential to show love and compassion and have the ability to make positive changes. Despite our shortcomings, God knows all of our sins and loves us unconditionally.

We may be inclined to categorize others as good or bad, but the reality is that there are no such absolutes. We all have our own stories and struggles. A person with a history of making wise choices can still fall prey to sin, and conversely, a person with a tarnished reputation can still find redemption through Jesus.

If you are feeling upset or frustrated by someone else's actions, remember that God loves them too. Instead of holding onto anger or resentment, try saying a prayer. Confide in God about your frustrations and thoughts on the matter; he already knows what you're thinking, so talk about it. We can always ask Him for a new perspective, guidance, or a change of heart. Love, in the end, is the solution to all conflicts.

Have a great day!

"'Teacher, which is the greatest commandment in the law?' Jesus said to him, 'You shall love the Lord your God with all your heart, with all your soul, and with all your mind.' This is the first and great commandment." Matthew 22:36-38

Good morning!

We are called to love God with all our hearts, souls, and minds. We should love Him for creating, providing, saving, forgiving, comforting, and everything He does for us. His fatherly love is greater than we can imagine, and He wants us to love Him with everything we have. But why does God want us to love Him with all of our hearts, soul, and mind?

Let's face it - God made everything, knows everything, and needs nothing. So, does He want us to love Him because of His big ego or the satisfaction of being loved? Absolutely not! He is not insecure or self-absorbed. He knows our purpose and our needs.

When we love God with all our hearts, we want to please Him and listen to what he has to say. We are willing to sacrifice our time and efforts to be with Him. Spending time with the Lord and obeying him can have a significant impact on our lives.

Moreover, when we love God with all our souls, we trust Him and believe what he says is true. With faith, we know that He has our best interest in mind, and we need not fear any difficulties or circumstances we may face. We can have security and confidence that He will see us through it.

Finally, when we love God with all our minds, we are content with any gift we receive from Him. Knowing that His gifts are thoughtful and given with love, we smile and rejoice for everything. We live our lives with gratitude and joy.

God does not want us to love Him because He needs it but because we do. So, love Him with all your heart, soul, and mind.

Have a great day!

"A second likewise is this, 'You shall love your neighbor as yourself.' The whole law and the prophets depend on these two commandments."
Matthew 22:39-40

Good morning!

In a world that can often feel harsh and divided, Jesus' message to love our neighbors as ourselves serves as a shining beacon, illuminating the path we all must follow. It's a divine commandment that we must take to heart.

As we learn to love God, our hearts are opened to His creation, and we become eager to serve Him by serving others. When we recognize that every person we encounter is a unique masterpiece, a reflection of God's image, we appreciate their worth.

Through this perspective, we can humbly seek out ways to help and care for everyone we meet, regardless of their background or behavior. Instead of expecting others to treat us a certain way or focusing on how they behave, we can shift our thoughts to our behavior or how we can make their lives a little brighter.

As we strive to better our lives, we can enrich others by giving what we hope to receive. If we want financial support for a project or a business, let's first offer support to others in need. If we seek a deeper relationship with God, let's help others learn and grow closer to Him.

Today, let's make a positive impact on those around us and choose to love our neighbors as ourselves.

Have a great day!

"But I tell you, love your enemies, bless those who curse you, do good to those who hate you, and pray for those who mistreat you and persecute you,"
Matthew 5:44

Good morning!

Loving those who mistreat us can be incredibly difficult, but it is exactly what Jesus calls us to do. He asks us to rise above hatred and respond with love, even in the face of adversity. It takes strength and courage to do what is right, especially when it feels like the world is against us.

Imagine you're driving down a road, and the person behind you gets angry, starts laying on the horn, and passes you. Our immediate response might be to get defensive or aggressive, but this only fuels the fire. Instead, what if we took a moment to acknowledge that we don't know what's happening in the other person's life or what their mental state might be? And when we next see them at a stoplight, we offer a genuine smile and wave.

It is important to listen to Jesus, not our worldly feelings, and to stand out by doing what is right. Loving those who mistreat us may be hard, but if we ask the Lord for strength, he will provide it. By representing Jesus and being a light in the darkness, we can show love even in the face of hatred.

Have a great day!

"Love is patient and is kind; love doesn't envy. Love doesn't brag, is not proud, doesn't behave itself inappropriately, doesn't seek its own way, is not provoked, takes no account of evil;" 1 Corinthians 13:4-5

Good morning!

In recent years, social media has become a powerful tool for connecting with others and sharing our experiences. However, it can also be a breeding ground for negativity and divisiveness. As we scroll through our news feeds, we may find ourselves comparing our lives to others, feeling inadequate or envious. We may also be confronted with opinions and beliefs that differ from our own, leading to frustration and anger.

But let us remember that love is the antidote to these negative emotions. We can choose to approach social media and all aspects of life with patience and kindness, treating others as we would want to be treated. We can choose to celebrate the successes and joys of others rather than comparing ourselves and feeling envious. And we can choose to respectfully engage with those who hold different opinions and beliefs, seeking to understand rather than to judge.

So let's demonstrate love in our interactions with others, both on and off social media. Being patient, kind, and humble, recognizing that we are all unique individuals with our own perspectives and experiences. And let's strive to build bridges rather than walls, fostering understanding and connection in a world that so desperately needs it.

Have a great day!

"doesn't rejoice in unrighteousness, but rejoices with the truth; bears all things, believes all things, hopes all things, endures all things." 1 Corinthians 13:6-7

Good morning!

Have you ever come across a wounded animal? I feel terrible when I see an animal in pain, and I cannot help but try to find a way to make them feel better. Usually, when they are hurt, they don't want anyone to come near them, whether it is a dog, cat, raccoon, bird, or turtle. They would try to bite, scratch, growl, or defend themselves in any possible way.

However, I endure their behavior, knowing that they don't understand my intentions, and I carefully help them in any way I can to get them out of their bad situation. Sometimes, they just need a little help getting to a safe place, while other times, they need more help than I can offer, so I need to call someone who can.

We should love others in the same way. We should bear and endure them at their weakest, meanest, and ugliest moments. We don't know what issues they are facing or the reasons for their attitudes. If we are capable, we should help them, but if it is beyond our abilities, we should call someone who can. We should always show kindness and compassion no matter what and leave the rest to God. We should pray for the people we cannot connect with, pray for cruel people, and pray about everything with hope and love.

Have a great day!

"And above all things be earnest in your love among yourselves, for love covers a multitude of sins." 1 Peter 4:8

Good morning!

We are reminded to be earnest in our love for one another, as love covers a multitude of sins. But how do we love and show kindness to those who don't share the same beliefs or values? For me, it can be challenging to be around people who use offensive language or behave in ways that go against godly principles.

However, when we feel challenged, we can turn to the example of Jesus, who showed love and forgiveness even to those who persecuted Him. As he hung on the cross, he prayed, "Father, forgive them, for they don't know what they are doing." (Luke 23:34)

Our task is not to judge or condemn but to show love, kindness, and patience to others. Love does not excuse their sinful behavior, but it does cover it.

We can choose to see past the flaws and mistakes of others and extend compassion and understanding.

God calls us to focus on loving Him and loving others, not on pointing out what's wrong with the world. It's not always easy, but with His guidance, we can choose to show love even in uncomfortable situations.

Have a great day!

"Put on therefore, as God's chosen ones, holy and beloved, a heart of compassion, kindness, lowliness, humility, and perseverance;" Colossians 3:12

Good morning!

I hope you woke up feeling refreshed and rejuvenated. It's not always easy to shake off a bad mood, but it's important to remember that we have the power to affect those around us. So, let's start the day off on the right foot!

It's okay to express our feelings, but it's important to do so in a way that doesn't spread negativity to those around us. When I'm feeling exhausted, I sometimes let it show on my face or in my tone, and it usually doesn't take long for me to see the same expression reflected back through my family. It's easy to get caught up in our own emotions, but it's important to take a step back and focus on the impact we're having on others.

Our actions, expressions, and words have the power to influence someone else's day. If we put a little effort into spreading kindness and love, we can reset the flow of the day and create a positive environment for ourselves and those around us.

So, let's not let our frustrations linger but put on a coat of compassion, kindness, lowliness, humility, and perseverance today, not just for our benefit but for the benefit of those around us.

Have a great day!

"But love your enemies, and do good, and lend, expecting nothing back; and your reward will be great, and you will be children of the Most High; for he is kind toward the unthankful and evil." Luke 6:35

Good morning!

Have you ever given a gift to someone knowing they may not appreciate it? In a world filled with judgment and where gratitude is not always guaranteed, giving a gift can feel daunting. We may fear that our efforts will be wasted or that we will be met with indifference. However, it's important to remember that the act of giving itself is an expression of love and care for others.

As we navigate through life, we will encounter those who have hurt or betrayed us. It's easy to close ourselves off and withhold our kindness and generosity from them. Yet, it is precisely in these moments that we are called to love our enemies and do good to those who have wronged us.

As this verse reminds us, we should be willing to lend a hand, offer thoughtful advice, and give in any way we can without expecting anything back. It takes courage and strength to extend compassion to those who oppose us. But by doing so, we can bring healing, reconciliation, and growth to ourselves and others.

So let's not be discouraged if our gifts go unappreciated. By loving our enemies, we are showing the same grace and kindness that God shows to us. Let's continue to give freely and love unconditionally to all.

Have a great day!

"He who doesn't love doesn't know God, for God is love." 1 John 4:8

Good morning!

Love. What is it anyway? Though it may be one of the most beautiful and inspiring words, we use it in English for a wide range of meanings. It describes a feeling that makes our hearts sing and brings joy to our lives. We also use the word "love" to describe things that we cherish, whether it's a cup of coffee, a family member, or a breathtaking sunrise. But what does love mean in a biblical sense?

According to 1 Corinthians 13:4-5, "Love is patient and is kind. Love doesn't envy. Love doesn't brag, is not proud, doesn't behave itself inappropriately, doesn't seek its own way, is not provoked, takes no account of evil." These qualities are not just emotions but also actions that we can take toward others to demonstrate our love.

The Bible tells us that God is love, and every beautiful and wonderful thing is born from it. When we're kind and patient with others, we're showing them a glimpse of God's unconditional love. On the other hand, when we're careless or short-tempered, we're failing to live up to God's standard of love.

It's easy to get caught up in our own needs and wants, but God calls us to serve and care for each other. When we prioritize the well-being of others and treat them with love, we embody God's love for us. Today, let's make a conscious effort to love others as God loves us - with selflessness, patience, and kindness.

Have a great day!

"For God so loved the world, that he gave his one and only Son, that whoever believes in him should not perish, but have eternal life." John 3:16

Good morning!

When I contemplate the nature of love, I am always drawn to this beautiful verse from the Bible, which reminds us of God's ultimate sacrifice. He loved the world so much that he gave his only Son as a sacrifice to save us from our sins.

This love is not just for a select few; it is available to anyone who believes in Him. No matter who you are, where you come from, or what you have done, God's love is for you. It is a love that transcends all barriers, a love that reaches the depths, and a love that gives us hope in the darkest of times.

It is a love that gave everything to save us, and it is a love that calls us to love others in the same way. We are called to love sacrificially, to put the needs of others before our own, and to love even our enemies.

So let's strive to love wholeheartedly, just as God has loved us without reservation, expectation, or hesitation. When we love as God loves, we bring light to the darkness, hope to the hopeless, and healing to the brokenhearted.

Have a great day!

"This I pray, that your love may abound yet more and more in knowledge and all discernment;"
Philippians 1:9

Good morning!

There is something beautiful about the way love grows when we truly get to know someone. The more we learn about them, the more we appreciate them and their unique qualities. We see them in a different light, and we begin to love them even more deeply.

I remember a colleague of mine who initially seemed strange and unapproachable. But as I got to know him better, I discovered his fascinating personality, and he became a dear friend. Our relationship flourished as we spent more time together, sharing stories and learning from each other.

This verse from Philippians reminds us that our love should always be growing and expanding, along with our knowledge and discernment. As we seek to understand God and his ways more profoundly, our love for Him will also increase. And as we learn more about others, we will come to appreciate their unique qualities and love them more deeply.

Let's pursue a life of continuous growth and love. Allowing our hearts to be filled with knowledge and understanding and fostering a love for others that flourishes with each passing day.

Have a great day!

"If you love those who love you, what credit is that to you? For even sinners love those who love them."
Luke 6:32

Good morning!

Jesus reminds us that merely loving those who love us is not enough. We must love and care for everyone, even those who may not be easy to love. We are called to love beyond what comes naturally, to see the beauty in each person, and to make an effort to understand and connect with them.

It can be challenging to love those who seem to enjoy pushing our buttons or those who have a bad reputation. But we must remember that we do not know their intentions, and everyone deserves love and compassion. Instead of avoiding them, we can surprise them with a friendly greeting or take the time to talk to them. By doing so, we might discover that they are just looking for attention or a friend.

We must care for the difficult people in our lives, not just the ones we enjoy being around. If we catch ourselves feeling annoyed or judgmental, we can remind ourselves that God is asking us to love them too. It takes patience and strength to care for those who are hard to be around, but it is what God calls us to do.

Today, remember to love beyond what comes naturally and care for those who might need it the most. Whether it's a smile from a distance, a listening ear, or a prayer for help, let's find it in our hearts to care.

Have a great day!

"If I then, the Lord and the Teacher, have washed your feet, you also ought to wash one another's feet." John 13:14

Good morning!

Have you ever gotten a pedicure? It's been years since I've had one, but I still remember feeling uncomfortable about someone else cleaning and taking care of my feet. I felt dirty and wanted to apologize for not taking better care of them. Even though it was their job, I had the urge to bend over and help scrub, file, and paint my nails with them.

When the pedicure was finished, I felt like a new person. It's funny how a pedicure can transform someone from feeling ashamed to feeling good about themselves. In the same way, Jesus takes any hurting, tired, and dirty person that comes to Him and makes them clean again.

This is exactly how Jesus treated his disciples and how he wants us to treat each other. He took them, just as they were, and lovingly washed their feet.

Can you imagine the dirt and grime on the feet of the men who had been walking tirelessly with Him? We must realize that we are not better than anybody else or too good for any job. We should remain humble and lovingly care for others.

Like a refreshing pedicure, we can make someone else feel good about themselves by simply caring. A kind gesture and a genuine smile go a long way.

Have a great day!

Breaking Free from Anxiety

FINDING PEACE WITHIN THE CHAOS

"I can do all things through Christ, who strengthens me." Philippians 4:13

Good morning!

A few years ago, I was preparing for a job interview and recited this verse to find the strength and courage I needed. I spent hours planning what to say, what to wear, and how to present myself. The thought of being judged and evaluated based on my answers was nerve-racking, and I began to doubt myself. I felt like I was wasting everyone's time and about to look foolish.

But then, I turned to God and recited this verse repeatedly while walking around the parking lot. Suddenly, God brought me to my knees, literally. I tripped and fell, tearing my pants and bleeding a little. Despite this, I found it hilarious - it was like God was playing an inside joke with me. It reminded me that the interview was just a moment in time, and I didn't need to get worked up about it. Worrying wouldn't change anything but my blood pressure.

My anxiety was replaced with amusement, and I was able to complete the interview with courage. I hope this verse brings you as much comfort as it does for me. God gives us strength and courage in unimaginable ways.

Have a great day!

"Haven't I commanded you? Be strong and courageous. Don't be afraid. Don't be dismayed, for Yahweh your God is with you wherever you go."
Joshua 1:9

Good morning!

God tells us to have courage and strength. He doesn't want us to fear obstacles or get nervous about new opportunities. He wants us to have faith and feel secure, knowing that He is with us wherever we go. This isn't a suggestion; He commands us to overcome our fears with strength and courage.

When I was in college, I had a public speaking class that required me to give a presentation. On the day of my scheduled speech, I became so nervous that I felt sick to my stomach. I kept telling myself that I couldn't do it and that I would make mistakes. I was a nervous wreck and talked myself right into skipping the class that day. Hoping that my professor would just fail me for that assignment, I showed up to the following class. To my surprise, she didn't get to my project yet, and I was the first person to be called up as soon as the class started.

I realized that I couldn't escape this difficult task. My heart pounded, and my hands shook as I walked up to the front of the room. I apologized for my nervousness but knew I had to face this difficult task. Shaking, stuttering, and barely able to speak above a whisper, I finally gave my presentation.

Looking back on that experience, I wonder how it would have gone if I had remembered that God was with me and that I had no reason to be afraid. Why did I believe my irrational thoughts over God's commands? It made me sick, it made me shake, and it affected my speech.

Today, if you're faced with a difficult choice, a tough conversation, or an intimidating task, I want to encourage you to pray about it. Keep God's commands to be strong and courageous in your mind. Don't try to escape what you're supposed to do. Whatever it is, you can do it with confidence because God is with you.

Have a great day!

"In nothing be anxious, but in everything, by prayer and petition with thanksgiving, let your requests be made known to God. And the peace of God, which surpasses all understanding, will guard your hearts and your thoughts in Christ Jesus." Philippians 4:6-7

Good morning!

In this verse, we are reminded not to be anxious about anything. This can be easier said than done, especially in today's world, where stress and uncertainty seem to be everywhere. However, the verse goes on to encourage us to bring our requests to God through prayer and thanksgiving. When we do this, we invite God's peace to fill our hearts and minds.

Do you feel like anxiety is a weakness of yours? Know that you are not alone. Many people struggle with anxiety, myself included. But the good news is that we don't have to face it alone. When we turn to God in prayer, He promises to guard our hearts and thoughts with a peace that surpasses all understanding.

So, the next time you feel anxious, remember to pray. Talk to God about your worries, your fears, your hopes, and your dreams. Ask Him for guidance and direction. And most importantly, thank Him for His presence in your life. As you do this, you will begin to experience His peace, which will give you the strength and courage to face whatever comes your way.

I pray that you will be filled with God's peace today and always. Remember, you are never alone, and with God by your side, you can overcome any obstacle that comes your way.

Have a great day!

"But whoever listens to me will dwell securely, and will be at ease, without fear of harm." Proverbs 1:33

Good morning!

Living in this world can be a scary and uncertain experience, with all the potential dangers surrounding us. From natural disasters to accidents and crime, there are countless ways in which we can be hurt or face harm. However, it's essential not to let fear take over our lives, as it can limit our ability to live fully and move forward.

While It's natural to want to protect ourselves and our loved ones, we cannot control everything. However, we can control our response to the challenges we face. When we pray and put our faith in God, we can find the courage and strength needed to overcome any obstacle.

God sees the big picture. He knows the trials and obstacles that will come our way, but He also knows how these experiences will shape us and help us grow. We may not always understand why certain things happen, but we can trust that God is always with us and will never leave us.

So, if you are feeling overwhelmed, take comfort in knowing that you have a loving God whose on your side. Take your worries to Him, and trust that He will guide you through whatever challenges come your way. With God by your side, you have nothing to fear.

Have a great day!

"Moses answered, 'But, behold, they will not believe me, nor listen to my voice; for they will say, "Yahweh has not appeared to you."'" Exodus 4:1

Good morning!

Have you ever faced a task that seemed too big to handle? Moses was in that situation when God called him to lead the Israelites out of Egypt. In Exodus 3:11, Moses asked God, "Who am I, that I should go to Pharaoh and bring the children of Israel out of Egypt?" Despite God's assurance that He would be with him, Moses still worried about what others would say.

God provided Moses with signs to prove that he was indeed sent by Him. He turned Moses' rod into a snake and back into a rod again, made his hand leprous, healed it, and promised to turn water into blood. However, despite all these signs, Moses still didn't feel adequate for the task. He made excuses about his speaking ability and begged God to find someone else.

God was patient with Moses but angry at his lack of trust. Ultimately, God allowed Aaron, Moses' brother, to help him. God wanted Moses to trust Him and do what he was supposed to, even if he was scared. This was Moses' calling, and he had to fulfill it.

If you feel inadequate for a task, tell God all your excuses and listen to what He has to say. He is all you need to help you overcome any difficulties, and He will not let you down.

Have a great day!

"Even though I walk through the valley of the shadow of death, I will fear no evil, for you are with me. Your rod and your staff, they comfort me."
Psalms 23:4

Good morning!

Last week, my daughter's room was extremely messy, making it difficult to walk around without stepping on something. Clothes and toys were scattered everywhere. As a mom, I asked her to clean up before doing anything else. However, she felt overwhelmed by the clutter and mess and thought it was impossible to clean it all up. After an hour, she was still sitting there, feeling hopeless and not doing anything. At that moment, I taught her the importance of redirecting her thoughts and not focusing on the mess she was in. I stayed with her, encouraged her, and talked to her as she cleaned her room. Before she knew it, the job was done.

Do you ever feel like you're stuck in a situation that seems too overwhelming to handle? It can be isolating and debilitating when all you see are mistakes, problems, and grief. However, God repeatedly tells us not to be afraid. If we focus on our problems instead of God, we will remain stuck and without hope.

Instead, choose to let God in. Pray about every worry and problem, and trust that He will take care of it. God is wonderful, and He will not leave you alone. He will guide you out of any circumstance.

Have a great day!

"Therefore don't be anxious for tomorrow, for tomorrow will be anxious for itself. Each day's own evil is sufficient." Matthew 6:34

Good morning!

Today is a gift, and we should make the most of it. Whether you have exciting plans or a regular work day, remember that every moment is precious. Don't waste your time worrying about the future because Jesus reminds us that we have enough to deal with in the present. He reminds us that birds and flowers don't worry about their basic needs, and if God takes care of them, He will surely take care of us as well.

Anxiety only steals our joy and wastes our time. Instead, trust in your Heavenly Father, who is always looking out for you. Let go of the things you can't control and focus on what's in front of you. Remember, each day has its own challenges, but with faith, we can overcome them.

So if you have a fun day planned, savor every moment and don't worry about tomorrow. And if you're facing a difficult task, take it one step at a time and leave tomorrow's worries for another day. Trust that your Heavenly Father has everything under control, and you can have peace in knowing that everything will be okay.

Have a great day!

"For you didn't receive the spirit of bondage again to fear, but you received the Spirit of adoption, by whom we cry, 'Abba! Father!'" Romans 8:15

Good morning!

Here we are reminded that as believers, we have not received a spirit of fear, but rather the Spirit of adoption, which allows us to call God our loving Father.

Life can be challenging, and at times we may feel lost, uncertain about our future, or fearful of our circumstances. We may even feel as though God is distant or unresponsive to our prayers. However, we can take comfort in knowing that we have been adopted into God's family and can approach Him with confidence, calling Him "Abba, Father."

Our Heavenly Father desires us to have faith in His plan for our lives, even when we don't understand our current situation. He doesn't want us to live in fear or feel alone. Instead, He invites us to cast our worries on Him and trust that He will take care of everything. Even on our most challenging days, we can find peace in God's love and goodness.

So always remember that you are never alone. God is with you every step of the way, and His love for you is beyond measure. Don't let fear hold you back; instead, call out to your Heavenly Father, and He will always be there to guide and comfort you.

Have a great day!

"For he wounds, and binds up. He injures, and his hands make whole. He will deliver you in six troubles; yes, in seven no evil shall touch you." Job 5:18-19

Good morning!

Have you ever experienced a time when everything seemed to be falling apart, and you were left wondering why it was happening? God has the power to both wound and heal, injure and make whole. It can be challenging to understand why we experience suffering and difficulties in life, but like Job, we can hold on to our faith and trust that God has a plan for our lives.

Even in challenging times, we can have hope for the future and trust that God is with us, guiding us through every obstacle and challenge. He can bring healing and restoration to our lives, even when it seems impossible.

If you are feeling down today, don't lose hope. Keep your faith in God, and trust in His infinite love and wisdom. He will deliver you from trouble and protect you from harm. Trust in Him, and you will overcome every obstacle that comes your way.

Have a great day!

"You therefore, my child, be strengthened in the grace that is in Christ Jesus." 2 Timothy 2:1

Good morning!

God's love for us is truly remarkable. He sent His only Son, Jesus Christ, to die for our sins and provided us with the gift of the Holy Spirit to walk with us throughout our lives. Through faith in Christ, we are given His grace - an undeserved kindness and favor that we could never earn on our own.

In this verse, Paul encourages Timothy to be strengthened in the grace that is in Christ Jesus. This is a powerful reminder that no matter what challenges we may face, we can find strength and comfort in God's grace. When we trust Him and believe that everything will work out according to His plan, we are empowered to face any circumstance with courage and hope.

So if you're feeling worried, anxious, or uncertain, take comfort in knowing God's grace is always available to you. You can't earn it, and you don't have to - it is a free gift that He offers to all who believe. Rest assured that no matter what happens, He is with you and will always provide the strength and grace you need.

Have a great day!

"Do you want to be made well?" John 5:6

Good morning!

In this story, Jesus went to a pool in Jerusalem where sick, disabled, and injured people had gathered to be healed. The pool was known for healing the first person to enter it after an angel would come down and stir it up. Interestingly, some versions of the Bible include John 5:4, while others omit it. Whatever the case may be, the man who was lying near the pool had been sick for thirty-eight years, and whenever the water moved, someone would jump in before he could.

Jesus knew that he had been sick for a long time, and his life would dramatically change if he were healed. This is also true for many of us. Some people struggle with their disabilities for so long that it becomes a normal way of life. If they were to be healed, it would feel new and uncomfortable. It's hard to learn how to live without a disability that you've become so accustomed to.

The same is true for any issues that we allow in our lives, such as smoking, drinking, drugs, food, shopping, and even emotional reactions. We know what's not good for us, but we are so comfortable with our crutch that we make it part of our lives. Maybe you think you want to quit something or start eating better, but not right now. Why not? Are you allowing yourself to become dependent on something that's holding you back?

After the sick man explained to Jesus that he couldn't get into the pool fast enough, Jesus said to him in John 5:8, "Arise, take up your mat, and walk." And he did. Can you imagine that? The anxiety and anticipation associated with a major change can be uncomfortable, but we can get past it. We can create a new normal in our lives if we truly want to change. We can find the strength we need with Jesus. How about you? Do you want to be made well?

Have a great day!

"Come to me, all you who labor and are heavily burdened, and I will give you rest." Matthew 11:28

Good morning!

As the day begins, I sometimes find myself feeling weighed down by the seemingly endless tasks on my to-do list. The pressure to get everything done quickly and efficiently can be overwhelming, but I know that the first step in managing this stress is to take a deep breath and prioritize my needs.

In times of stress and uncertainty, it is crucial to turn to our faith and put God first. By taking the time to pray and thanking Him for all that He does in our lives, we can find peace and guidance amid our struggles. In those moments of prayer, we can express our worries and seek His help where we need it most.

When we feel overwhelmed, it can be all too easy to focus solely on our own needs and tasks, neglecting our relationships with others. But it's important to remember that our priorities should always include loving God and loving others. Let's strive to treat others with kindness and patience, even when we're busy.

Have a great day!

"I have put my trust in God. I will not be afraid. What can man do to me?" Psalms 56:11

Good morning!

These words are a powerful reminder that we have nothing to fear when we have faith in God. We may encounter obstacles, difficulties, and challenges in life, but we must remember that the one who created the universe is faithful to those who love him. He will grant us the strength, perseverance, and wisdom to overcome any situation.

We often magnify our trivial matters, but with God, nothing is impossible. He holds the mysteries of the universe and the intricacies of every molecule and organism, and his ways surpass our understanding. Have you ever marveled at the complexity of cells, the vastness of space, or the tiniest microbe? There is so much beauty and wonder around us, which we cannot fully comprehend, yet we know that our Creator has designed it all.

Regardless of what we are going through, whether it's a momentous challenge or a mundane routine, God sees us. He is with us in our darkest hour, in our toughest battles, and in our everyday lives. He wants us to trust in Him, lean on Him, and rest in His grace. He loves us deeply and cares for each one of us uniquely.

Although the Earth is a mere speck in the universe, and you're just one person among billions of people on this planet, you are so very special to God. Knowing His love for us, we can face the day with courage, walk by faith, and embrace the fact that we have an all-powerful God who is always by our side.

Have a great day!

"Peace I leave with you. My peace I give to you; not as the world gives, give I to you. Don't let your heart be troubled, neither let it be fearful." John 14:27

Good morning!

If you find yourself overwhelmed with anxiety and worry, it may be time to refocus your thoughts. Remember that the peace Jesus left for you is always within you. Do not let your worries obscure this truth. Instead, fix your eyes on God's strength and stay on track to complete your tasks.

As a child, I used to cry over minor cuts and scrapes. My older brother would come over, look at my injury, and then pinch me. Though not the kindest method, his point was valid. I stopped fixating on my injury and refocused my thoughts on where he pinched me. Suddenly, my injury no longer mattered. Our thoughts are powerful, shaping how we perceive our circumstances.

If we choose to let go of our anxiety, we can navigate our troubles with a calm mind. The peace He gives is not of this world, but it's the same peace that Jesus himself had while he faced temptations, endured pain, and encountered difficult people and circumstances. It's a peace that surpasses all human understanding, and if He could remain tranquil in this world, then so can we.

Don't lose sight of this truth, and let your fears hold you back. Jesus wants you to live a life overflowing with peace, love, and joy.

Have a great day!

The Freedom of Forgiveness

LETTING GO AND MOVING FORWARD

"David said to God, 'I have sinned greatly, in that I have done this thing. But now put away, I beg you, the iniquity of your servant, for I have done very foolishly.'" 1 Chronicles 21:8

Good morning!

Like David, I, too, have sinned and made mistakes in my life. At times, I feel ashamed and unworthy of God's forgiveness. However, it is essential to remember that God's love for us is unconditional and boundless. He already knows all of our faults and failures, yet He still chooses to forgive us and offer us a fresh start.

Jesus sacrificed his life to save us from our sins. He allowed us to be reconciled and have a new life in Him. Regardless of the number or severity of our sins, His sacrifice was enough to cover them all, and His forgiveness is available to us all through Jesus Christ.

Therefore, if you feel weighed down by your past mistakes and the burden of your sins, don't lose hope. Simply surrender your sinful life to Jesus, and He will give you His. You can start today with a clean slate and a renewed spirit.

Remember that you're precious and valuable in God's eyes. He views you as beautiful, forgiven, and loved. Accept His forgiveness and be filled with hope, joy, and purpose.

Have a great day!

"For him who knew no sin he made to be sin on our behalf; so that in him we might become the righteousness of God." 2 Corinthians 5:21

Good morning!

Can you Imagine for a moment having a dog you dearly love, regularly take for walks, and play at a dog park? One day, as your beloved dog played at the park, he suddenly spotted a stranger that he thought was threatening and ferociously attacked him. While you can understand your dog's intentions and forgive him, the event happened, and his actions will have consequences. Although your dog may be sweet and dear to you, he could potentially face the consequences of his actions, such as being put down.

Similarly, our mistakes and sins deserve punishment, and even though God dearly loves us, He is holy and just. The stains of our sins keep us separate from our beautiful and almighty God, and there is nothing we can do to escape the consequences. Only God can fix the mess we've created.

However, God had a plan to fix the mess we've created. Instead of letting us pay the price for our mistakes, Jesus took our place. His suffering on the cross wasn't just the wounds from man; it was our eternal punishment. We were released from our debts and washed clean.

Today, we don't have to walk with our heads hanging down for our poor decisions. Jesus took our sins and made them his. When we follow Him, we don't have to be afraid of not being accepted; we are given confidence in knowing where we stand with God. We can thank the Lord for forgiving our sins, pick ourselves up, and walk boldly, glorifying Him and spreading the good news.

Have a great day!

"All who heard him were amazed, and said, "Isn't this he who in Jerusalem made havoc of those who called on this name? And he had come here intending to bring them bound before the chief priests!" Acts 9:21

Good morning!

Do you remember the incredible transformation of the apostle Paul, who went from persecuting Christians to becoming one of the most influential leaders in spreading the gospel? His story is a testament to the power of change and the fantastic things that can happen when we encounter the love of Christ.

Before his conversion, Paul was known as Saul, a man who threatened and tortured followers of Jesus. But on a journey near Damascus, he encountered a blinding light and heard the voice of Jesus, asking him, "Saul, Saul, Why do you persecute me?" At that moment, Paul's life was forever changed. Since he lost his sight, the other men traveling with him led him to Damascus, where he fasted and waited for three days until a man named Ananias, who was sent by God, came to restore his sight and baptize him.

Paul's transformation was so remarkable that even those who knew him were amazed. They couldn't believe he was the same man who had caused so much trouble for Christians in Jerusalem. But through God's grace, Paul was able to turn his life around and become a powerful advocate for the gospel.

Can you imagine forgiving someone so evil and even accepting them as part of your family? His story teaches us that no one is beyond redemption; and that even the most unlikely people can be transformed by God. We, too, can be changed by encountering Christ and become instruments of His love and grace to those around us.

Have a great day!

"If we confess our sins, he is faithful and righteous to forgive us the sins, and to cleanse us from all unrighteousness." 1 John 1:9

Good morning!

Reflecting on the purpose of confessing my sins to God, I thought about the importance of saying I am sorry. From an early age, we are often taught to apologize for anything we did that hurt or upset someone else. Whether it was intentional or not, saying sorry is still a polite and meaningful gesture. But why is that? Is it to make the other person feel better or us?

I once had a close relative steal something from me. It was a handmade, unique item that went missing, and I later saw them with it. Although the item wasn't valuable, and I could live without it, the thought of them taking something from me was surprising and hurtful. I asked where she got it from, but she couldn't remember or didn't want to admit her actions. Although I will always love her, I still think about what she did. If she had confessed or explained herself, I would have been so happy that she had the courage to tell me. It would have shown that she valued our relationship more than her comfort. Our relationship would have been much stronger with honesty.

Likewise, when we confess our sins to God, we show Him that we value our relationship with Him more than our comfort or pride. We acknowledge our wrongdoing and seek His forgiveness. Even though God already knows our sins, confessing them allows us to be honest with Him and take responsibility for our actions. We can trust that when we confess, God is faithful and righteous to forgive us and cleanse us from all unrighteousness, as stated in 1 John 1:9.

Unlike earthly fathers who may demand retribution for what we've done, God does not require us to make amends or pay for our sins. Jesus paid the price in full on the cross, and through Him, we are forgiven and made righteous in God's eyes. Hallelujah!

Have a great day!

"For I will be merciful to their unrighteousness. I will remember their sins and lawless deeds no more." Hebrews 8:12

Good morning!

After asking for forgiveness, do you feel forgiven? Sometimes, even after confessing our sins and seeking God's forgiveness, we still feel sorrowful. We continue to remember and replay our past mistakes, feeling remorseful about them. We may even find ourselves asking for forgiveness repeatedly for the same sins, but who are we really asking?

When God forgives our sins, He does not bring them up again. It is over and done with. Unlike people who bring up past offenses during disagreements, God forgets they ever happened. Therefore, there is no reason for us to ask for forgiveness repeatedly for the same sins. By doing so, we could be questioning whether our sins were actually forgiven, or maybe we are double-checking to ensure we remembered every part of the apology. Perhaps we need to apologize to someone else, or we may need to ask ourselves for forgiveness.

At times, we might be ashamed of something we did or maybe something we should have done. Sometimes, we might feel guilty about things we allowed to happen or even things that were done to us that we had no control over. No matter what the sin is, if you're feeling guilty about something today, talk to your heavenly Father. Ask God for forgiveness, change your ways, and you will be forgiven.

Then, be sure to forgive yourself. Although you may not forget your errors, you don't need to bring them up over and over again. Reliving the situation with shame only causes harm to yourself. Instead, leave the past behind and move forward with the grace given to you by God. Today is a new day, and you can be a new person. Let go of the past and embrace the new.

Have a great day!

"Therefore putting away falsehood, speak truth each one with his neighbor. For we are members of one another." Ephesians 4:25

Good morning!

As we reflect on forgiveness, let's not underestimate the value of speaking truthfully. It can be all too easy to react in the heat of the moment and say or do things that we later come to regret, especially with those closest to us. However, when we let our emotions take control, we risk unintentionally causing harm to those around us. When that happens, it's crucial to acknowledge our mistakes and take responsibility for our actions, even if it's not easy.

Honesty is the cornerstone of healthy relationships. It takes bravery and humility to admit our faults and ask for forgiveness, but it's vital for our growth and healing.

If you're grappling with feelings of guilt or shame over something you've done, I urge you to pray and seek guidance from God. He can offer you the strength and wisdom necessary to approach those you've hurt and extend a heartfelt apology.

Remember, the Bible teaches us to reconcile with one another and to love even those with whom we may not see eye-to-eye. When we make mistakes, it's important to speak the truth, seek forgiveness, and demonstrate love to others. Let's continue to strive for honesty and integrity in our relationships while being quick to forgive and seek forgiveness.

Have a great day!

"bearing with one another, and forgiving each other, if any man has a complaint against any; even as Christ forgave you, so you also do." Colossians 3:13

Good morning!

Let's take a moment to talk about the small things. The things that irritate us or get under our skin, like someone chewing loudly at dinner or a stranger reaching around us to grab an item while shopping. It's easy to get frustrated or offended by these minor inconveniences, but Jesus calls us to bear with one another and extend grace.

It's important to recognize that the actions of others are not always intentional and may not be directed toward us personally. Instead of allowing ourselves to become agitated or angry, let's practice giving grace as freely as our Heavenly Father does.

When we feel hurt or slighted by someone, we can choose to forgive them and give them the benefit of the doubt. Maybe they are unaware that their behavior is bothering us, or perhaps they are struggling with their own challenges. Whatever the case may be, we can follow the example of Christ and forgive as we have been forgiven.

So let's strive to be patient and kind toward others, even in the small things. As Colossians 3:13 teaches us, "Even as Christ forgave you, so you also do."

Have a great day!

"looking carefully lest there be any man who falls short of the grace of God; lest any root of bitterness springing up trouble you and many be defiled by it;" Hebrews 12:15

Good morning!

Can you think of someone who exemplifies bitterness? Perhaps they come across as cold, harsh, and critical toward others or themselves. Bitterness often stems from holding onto past offenses. If we fail to let go and move on, it lingers in our minds, simmering throughout the day or even longer. This can lead to bubbling anger, judgment, resentment, frustration, and more. Being around a bitter person is challenging, as they unknowingly can steal the smiles right off of the faces they're around.

Just last week, I was frustrated over something so trivial that I can't even recall what it was. Nevertheless, I didn't let it go immediately. Instead, I dwelled on it and became a snappy and difficult person to be around. When my husband asked me what was bothering me, I denied having any problems, and as I went about my day, my frustration escalated. I started nitpicking at messes, bringing up issues that needed to be fixed, and my perception of everything around me became negatively skewed.

Shortly after, my kids became irritable and threw tantrums. Their bright and playful morning turned into a day filled with meltdowns and tears. That's when it hit me—I had allowed this negativity to permeate our home. Due to my inability to let go of my problems, I carried that weight around and spread it like a contagious virus.

Friends, it's crucial to forgive and to do so quickly. Everyone experiences hurt, disappointment, and frustration at times, but if you don't release the things that bother you, they will take root, grow, and ultimately make you a bitter person. So today, let's choose to let it go, cut out the negativity, and embrace the day that God has given us.

Have a great day!

"for all have sinned, and fall short of the glory of God;" Romans 3:23

Good morning!

A few days ago, while I was praying, I wanted to ask the Lord for forgiveness for my sins, but I couldn't think of a single thing I had done wrong. Embarrassed, I asked God to forgive me for not knowing where I was falling short and to help me understand my sins.

I started reading through the Bible, scanning articles, and watching videos in search of a simple explanation of sins, but I only grew more confused. That was until I discovered that the Hebrew and Greek words translated as "sin" throughout the Bible were often defined as an offense, failing, and missing the mark (Bible Tools 1992; Benner, 1999; Bible Project, 2018). These words were frequently used in archery to describe missing the target. As an archer, I can easily relate to and visualize that concept.

In archery, you might have trouble hitting the target when you first start, but with practice and effort, you will eventually hit it. Everyone has different abilities and starting points, so archers usually don't judge their success by comparing their scores to others. The only comparison that makes sense is how you're shooting now compared to how you started, but there's always room for improvement. Even if you're a good shot and hit the bullseye many times, you can always move the target further back.

I learned that even on my best day, I don't come close to where I am supposed to be. I may be hitting the paper target but not the x in the center. Somedays, I may shoot too far to the left with pride; other days, I shoot a little to the right with judgment, and then there are days when I don't know where my arrow went.

It's great to be excited about achieving your personal best, but when you do, it's time to fine-tune and set new goals. Whatever you're working on today, stand firm, adjust your grip, and shoot straight.

Have a great day!

"As for you, you meant evil against me, but God meant it for good, to bring to pass, as it is today, to save many people alive." Genesis 50:20

Good morning!

Have you ever been disappointed in God? Sometimes we wonder why God allows horrible things to happen. Some days can be met with tears and confusion; we might wonder why He doesn't prevent these types of suffering. But in the midst of our pain, we can find comfort in the fact that God can turn even the most evil acts into something good.

One example of this is in the story of Joseph, the dream interpreter. As you may recall, Joseph was a boy fascinated with dreams. His dad thought he was pretty special and gave him a colorful coat. However, his brothers were jealous and plotted to kill him. Thankfully, they decided to sell him and pretend he was dead instead.

Later, Joseph was brought to Egypt and sold to one of the Pharaoh's officers. While working, his master's wife tried to seduce him but he managed to run away. She falsely accused him of trying to sleep with her, which sent Joseph to prison.

Years went by, and one day, the Pharaoh had a few crazy dreams and he desperately wanted to know their meaning. Joseph was able to tell him the interpretations that God had given him. Pleased with his answer, Pharaoh appointed him to rule over everyone but Pharaoh himself.

In that position, God used Joseph to save many lives during a widespread famine. Even Joseph's cruel brothers came to buy food out of desperation. Instead of giving them what they deserved, Joseph forgave them. He knew that God used every cruelty for the greater good.

If you're feeling disappointed, upset, or hurt, remember that God hasn't left you, and His plans are always for the good. As Joseph's story shows us, God can take even the most painful situations and turn them into something beautiful.

Have a great day!

"Jesus said to him, "I don't tell you until seven times, but, until seventy times seven." Matthew 18:22

Good morning!

How many times should we forgive someone? According to Jesus, seventy times seven. That means forgiving someone for not responding to our greeting, forgiving them for being rude or hurtful, forgiving them for spreading rumors or laughing at our mistakes, and forgiving them even when they hurt us many times in a day.

We are called to forgive often and quickly. When we hold onto grudges, we allow the offense to continue to hurt us and consume our thoughts. This can prevent us from accomplishing our goals and negatively affect those around us. God wants us to let go of the offense and free ourselves from the pain and negative emotions it brings. Whether it's a big or small offense, we must forgive the person who hurt us.

Today, let's forgive quickly and completely, just as God forgives us. Remember, forgiveness is not always easy and may require forgiveness by faith, not just by how we feel. But with God's help, we can let go of the hurt and move forward in peace.

Have a great day!

"He said to him, "Lord, I am ready to go with you both to prison and to death!" Luke 22:33

Good morning!

No matter how close we are to someone, they are bound to disappoint us. Unfortunately, we are all tempted and may inadvertently do or say things that cause pain to others. That is why we should have faith in no one or anything other than God, as we will only be let down.

Even though we do not intend to hurt those we love, we all make mistakes. Whether it is something said in the heat of an argument or a personal choice that affects the family, we must learn to address the issue and forgive one another.

This verse is a prime example of a person who did not think they would ever betray someone they loved. Here, Peter declares that he would follow Jesus anywhere, but Jesus knew and pointed out that Peter would deny knowing him. Not only once but three times before the rooster crows.

We often say things like, "I would never do that!" or hear parents say, "My kids would never do that." However, like Peter, who denied Jesus, we are often proven wrong. As the old saying goes, "Never say never." We do not know what circumstances will come our way or what battles others are fighting. It is important to remember that we are all imperfect people and that we need to forgive just as much as we need forgiveness.

Have a great day!

"But if you don't forgive men their trespasses, neither will your Father forgive your trespasses."
Matthew 6:15

Good morning!

Today, let's talk about something that many of us struggle with: forgiveness. Take a moment and think, is there someone in your life whom you find it difficult to forgive? Perhaps someone who has hurt you deeply or wronged you in some way? It's not easy, but it's essential to address and overcome the issue of unforgiveness.

It's like clutter in a closet that needs to be cleaned out when we hold onto unforgiveness. It can be tempting to ignore it, but the longer we ignore it, the more it continues to hurt us and those around us. The Bible reminds us that if we don't forgive others, our heavenly Father won't forgive us.

Forgiveness doesn't mean that we excuse what someone has done, but it means that we release them and ourselves from the torment and recurring hurt. It may seem impossible to forgive someone who doesn't deserve forgiveness, but that's where grace comes in. God wants us to overcome what has been done and give them the same grace He gives us. We need to extend mercy and forgiveness, just as Jesus did for us when He sacrificed Himself on the cross.

If you're struggling to forgive someone, take it to God. Let Him know that you want to forgive them but can't do it alone. Ask Him to help you release the pain and resentment and replace it with His love and peace. Remember that forgiveness is not just for the other person but also for our healing and freedom.

Have a great day!

"Therefore be merciful, even as your Father is also merciful. Don't judge, and you won't be judged. Don't condemn, and you won't be condemned. Set free, and you will be set free." Luke 6:36-37

Good morning!

Today, as we wrap up our discussion on forgiveness, I want to ask: Are you still carrying the weight of the past? Do you find yourself feeling hurt whenever you share your story or dwell on past issues? If so, it may be time to set yourself free.

It's easy to fall into the trap of judgment and blame. We may focus on how we were raised, what we lacked, the wrongs done to us, and the challenges we faced. However, life is dynamic, and things change. People change, perspectives evolve, and circumstances transform.

This morning, I realized that my past is filled with stories I often would bring up. I talked about my history when I felt the need to showcase my experiences or to remind myself of who I am and where I came from. Unbeknownst to me, I was keeping my wounds open and savoring the bitterness. I hadn't genuinely forgiven as I thought I had. Deep down, I was still accusing others of their poor decisions. But who am I to judge? Only God has the authority to pass judgment on His creation.

Today, we can make a conscious decision to stop condemning and rehashing issues that do not need to be revisited. We can choose to forgive all past offenses and leave them where they belong—in the past. We can set them free and allow our wounds to heal.

God can, and often does, take things that were once harmful and transform them into something good. The past can serve as a reference point to help others through their struggles, and any scars can serve as a testament to healing and overcoming. Let's choose to let the past go, and set it free so that we can experience a new kind of freedom.

Have a great day!

Embracing Gratitude

DISCOVERING ABUNDANCE IN THE BLESSINGS OF LIFE

"As they were eating, Jesus took bread, gave thanks for it, and broke it. He gave to the disciples, and said, 'Take, eat; this is my body.'" Matthew 26:26

Good morning!

During their meal together, a special moment unfolded. Jesus, the embodiment of selfless love, took the bread into His hands. Yet, He did not simply distribute it; instead, He paused to give thanks. In that single act, He revealed the depth of His gratitude, knowing that His body would soon be broken for us all.

In the Scriptures, it says: "But He was pierced for our transgressions. He was crushed for our iniquities. The punishment that brought our peace was on Him, and by His wounds, we are healed" (Isaiah 53:5). These words demonstrate the magnitude of His sacrifice. Jesus willingly bore the weight of our sins, allowing His body to be pierced and crushed so we could find forgiveness and redemption.

Today, let's not get too comfortable with our daily routines that we forget the magnitude of His selfless love. Let's remember the bread broken by Jesus, a symbol of His sacrifice, and let it remind us to be grateful for gifts that seem ordinary but are truly extraordinary. Let's take the time to give thanks not just before meals or during communion but for all things. May He transform our hearts and let them overflow with gratitude.

Have a great day!

"I will give thanks to Yahweh with my whole heart. I will tell of all your marvelous works. I will be glad and rejoice in you. I will sing praise to your name, O Most High." Psalms 9:1-2

Good morning!

In our lives, it's easy to fall into the habit of focusing on what we lack. We see people with nice cars, fancy clothes, beautiful homes, and seemingly perfect families everywhere we look. As we notice what others have that we don't, we can begin to imagine that their lives must be easier, happier, and better than ours.

These thoughts can be like weeds in a garden, quickly spreading and crowding out the beautiful plants we desire to flourish. We must weed out the invasive and thorny thoughts that overshadow our blessings. By doing so, we can nurture and cultivate the good things in our lives.

The key is to appreciate what we have so that we don't lose sight of our own blessings.

When we cultivate genuine gratitude for the good and beautiful things in our lives, we won't be preoccupied with what others possess. Instead, we'll be too busy thanking God for His abundant provision.

As we start the day, let's praise God for everything he has done in our lives. Whether it's a loving relationship that many pray for, a healthy body that enables us to live fully, a caring family, or even the simple gift of water to quench our thirst, let's give Him thanks. We don't need more things to be happy; we only need more gratitude for what we have and faith that God will provide what we need.

So let's follow the psalmist's example and give thanks to God with our whole hearts, telling of all His marvelous works. Let's be glad and rejoice in Him, singing praises to His name.

Have a great day!

"In everything give thanks, for this is the will of God in Christ Jesus toward you." 1 Thessalonians 5:18

Good morning!

As we start a new day, let's take a moment to appreciate the beauty and wonder of everything around us. From the gentle breeze to the shimmering sun, there is so much to be grateful for. Let's embrace the gift of life and be thankful for all that we have been blessed with.

Starting our day with a spirit of gratitude can set the tone for the rest of our day. We can choose to focus on the small things that bring us joy, the kind gestures of others, and the intricate details of the world around us. When we appreciate the beauty in our midst, we open ourselves up to the abundance of blessings that surround us.

However, as the day progresses, it is natural for little frustrations to arise. Maybe we spill coffee on our new shirt, or we get stuck in traffic, or we receive an unwelcome piece of news. In those moments, it can be easy to become consumed by negative thoughts and forget the blessings that still abound.

But here's the beautiful truth: God can use every experience for the greater good. What may seem like a setback or a disappointment may actually be a catalyst for growth, learning, and change. We can trust that God has a plan for our lives and that even when things don't go as we hoped or expected, He is still working all things together for the greater good.

So, my dear friend, let's choose to be grateful today and every day. Let's give thanks for the beauty that surrounds us, the love that sustains us, and the hope that inspires us. Let's trust that God is with us every step of the way.

Have a great day!

"Immediately he received his sight and followed him, glorifying God. All the people, when they saw it, praised God." Luke 18:43

Good morning!

In Luke 18:43, we witness a beautiful moment of healing and faith. Despite being told to be quiet, a blind man called out to Jesus and asked for mercy. He was granted the gift of sight through his unwavering determination and faith. It's hard to imagine the overwhelming gratitude he must have felt, and the people who witnessed the miracle couldn't help but praise God.

But what happens after the miracle is just as important. The man who had his sight restored didn't just walk away - he became a follower of Jesus, glorifying God with his newfound gift. It's easy to think we would do the same, but how often do we take the blessings we've been given for granted and fail to use them to honor God?

As we go about our lives, we're surrounded by countless gifts from God - the ability to see, hear, speak, a roof over our heads, food on our tables, and so much more. Yet, too often, we focus on what we don't have instead of what we do. We compare ourselves to others and feel like we're missing out instead of recognizing the unique and special gifts God has crafted just for us.

Let's take a moment to appreciate the thoughtfulness and care that went into each and every one of God's gifts. Let's honor Him by using those gifts to glorify Him and bring joy to those around us. And above all, remember to thank our Father in Heaven for the blessings that surround us daily.

Have a great day!

"'But now we have lost our appetite. There is nothing at all except this manna to look at.'"
Numbers 11:6

Good morning!

Imagine the weariness that comes from eating the same leftovers over and over again. Now, multiply that feeling by 40 years. It's no wonder the Israelites became prone to complaining, murmuring, and doubting God's provision. They longed for variety and even thought it would have been better to remain as the enslaved people they were in Egypt.

God, however, was not pleased with their murmuring. Despite their complaints, He continued to supply all their needs. He provided manna for them to eat, fresh water to quench their thirst, and when they craved meat, He sent quail their way. Yet, they failed to recognize that no matter their circumstances, they could trust God's faithfulness.

Reflecting on my own experiences, I recall a time when my family faced financial struggles. We had very little money, and I remember a week when all we had to eat was soup. Each night, the soup seemed to become more watered down and less appetizing. I found myself complaining and desiring a change.

Looking back on that situation now, I am grateful for the experience. At that moment, I was solely focused on the taste of our food and longed for something different. Yet, I never had to worry about going hungry. My mother remained faithful and thanked the Lord for our meals, never showing discouragement. Even when we had nothing else, she faithfully added water and bouillon cubes to the pot. It taught us the importance of finding reasons to be grateful in all circumstances.

If you find yourself struggling to see beyond the wilderness, remember to trust in God and express gratitude. He will guide you through the challenges and provide for your needs. Just as He led the Israelites through the wilderness, He will also lead you.

Have a great day!

"For though the fig tree doesn't flourish, nor fruit be in the vines; the labor of the olive fails, the fields yield no food; the flocks are cut off from the fold, and there is no herd in the stalls: yet I will rejoice in Yahweh. I will be joyful in the God of my salvation!" Habakkuk 3:17-18

Good morning!

As I woke up this morning and looked at the beautiful sunrise, I couldn't help but praise God for the magnificent masterpiece I had the privilege to see. He doesn't limit his gifts to the deserving, the grateful, or any particular class of people. He extends the wonders of his creation to all, allowing everyone, everywhere, the opportunity to experience what he has made.

I praise God for who he is, not just for what he does for me. He is the great I AM, the Almighty, the potter, the author of life who created so much out of nothing. No one can comprehend the complexity of his work or fathom the wonders of life. He is worthy of praise in all circumstances and situations.

When we consider the mysteries of this world that we have yet to uncover, the vastness of galaxies and beyond, and the order in which God structured every cell, it's natural to feel humbled and speechless. Let's remain filled with joy for knowing who God is and for the love, hope, and listening ear He offers us.

God, we thank you for loving us and for the hope you provide. Please help us to maintain our joy and to continually praise you for who you are. Amen.

Have a great day!

"For everything there is a season, and a time for every purpose under heaven: a time to be born, and a time to die; a time to plant, and a time to pluck up that which is planted; a time to kill, and a time to heal; a time to break down, and a time to build up; a time to weep, and a time to laugh; a time to mourn, and a time to dance;" Ecclesiastes 3:1-4

Good morning!

Yesterday, while brushing my daughter's teeth, I noticed a new tooth coming up behind one of her baby teeth. I wanted to cry. She is growing up so fast, and I just want to stop time for a while. Why can't I keep her as the sweet, innocent girl she is right now? Life is so precious and ever-changing. This change is not a big deal, but at the same time, it is life-changing. Soon I will never get to see that same baby tooth smile. This season is approaching an end, and a new one will begin.

This is a little reminder for me that every single day is special. Within the long nights, tired days, endless work, and minor frustrations, there is beauty everywhere. People will come and go, houses will be built and torn down, trees will be planted and burned, and nothing on earth will stay the same. Through repetition, we tend to get comfortable and forget to be thankful for all the little things in life. It's easy to miss the leaves changing right in front of our eyes, but they are. One day we might miss the very things that get on our nerves. For me, I just realized that even though brushing my daughter's teeth isn't my favorite thing to do, I'll miss brushing those little baby teeth.

I thank God that He let me experience all things that I take for granted. Thank God for every season, every day, every person, and every moment He gives you. You never know what today will bring or even if you'll be here tomorrow. Make it a great day to be alive and appreciate those around you.

Have a great day!

"Jesus answered, 'Weren't the ten cleansed? But where are the nine?'" Luke 17:17

Good morning!

As Jesus journeyed toward Jerusalem, ten lepers came to Him from a distance, calling out, "Jesus, Master, have mercy on us!" Upon seeing them, He instructed, "Go and show yourselves to the priests." They were healed as they obeyed and began to make their way to the priests.

This account teaches us a valuable lesson on obedience, faith, and trust. The lepers did not hesitate, question, or doubt Jesus' words but simply obeyed His command. In doing so, they were rewarded with miraculous healing.

However, this story is also a reminder of the importance of expressing gratitude to God. In Luke 17:15-19, we read of how only one of the ten lepers, a Samaritan, returned to give thanks and glorify God for his healing. Jesus questioned the whereabouts of the other nine, who failed to give glory to God and acknowledge the source of their blessings.

Sometimes, in our eagerness to enjoy our gifts, we forget to be thankful. We can become so consumed with our own happiness that we neglect to acknowledge the source and express our gratitude to God. Let's not be like the nine lepers who forgot to give thanks but instead, be like the one who returned to give glory to God.

So, as we go about our day, let's remember to obey God's commands, have faith, trust in Him, and most importantly, express our gratitude for His countless blessings in our lives.

Have a great day!

"Each of you not just looking to his own things, but each of you also to the things of others."
Philippians 2:4

Good morning!

Do you truly appreciate the people in your life? It's easy to say we do, but how often do we actually express our gratitude?

Reflecting on my own life, I realized that while I am grateful for my loved ones, I often fail to show my appreciation for the things they do. I don't thank my husband for taking care of the vehicles or my children for their help around the house. I don't express gratitude to my coworkers for their hard work and support.

This lack of appreciation can cause us to take others for granted and even expect them to behave in certain ways without acknowledging their efforts. But gratitude is an essential aspect of our relationships with others and with God.

When we show gratitude, we build others up and encourage them to continue their acts of kindness. It's also a way to glorify God, who gives us all the ability to serve and care for one another. By thanking others, we acknowledge their good works and the love they bring into our lives.

So let's make a conscious effort to express our gratitude to those around us, not just for the big things, but for the everyday acts of kindness that often go unnoticed. Let's thank God for the people in our lives and look for ways to show that we care.

Have a great day!

"But about midnight Paul and Silas were praying and singing hymns to God, and the prisoners were listening to them." Acts 16:25

Good morning!

In the middle of the night, Paul and Silas found themselves confined within the cold walls of a prison cell. Stripped of their freedom and enduring the pain of physical wounds, they faced a daunting situation. However, their response to this adversity teaches us a powerful lesson about the strength and resilience that comes from an unwavering faith in God.

Instead of succumbing to despair or allowing bitterness to take hold, Paul and Silas turned to prayer and worship. While in chains, they lifted their voices and sang praises to God. They chose to focus their attention on Him and His goodness instead of their suffering. As they sang praises to Him, their voices echoed throughout the prison walls and reached the ears of their fellow prisoners.

Can you imagine what they might have thought? Maybe they were surprised by Paul and Silas's ability to find gratitude in their difficult situation, or perhaps they thought they were just a couple of nuts making a lot of noise. Either way, I'm guessing they had no idea of the transformative power that a steadfast faith in God has. That is, until they witnessed it firsthand.

While they listened to the songs that flowed from Paul and Silas's mouths, not only could they hear the comfort and strength in their voices, but they could also feel the earthquake under their feet, see the doors fly open, and witness the chains loosen. Needless to say, it was a life-changing experience for everyone in that prison.

Like Paul and Silas, when we face our challenges in life, we can look for reasons to be grateful and lift our voices in praise, knowing that our worship is not dependent on our surroundings but on the unchanging character of God. With steadfast faith, He can transform our hearts and the hearts of those around us.

Have a great day!

"At that time, Jesus answered, 'I thank you, Father, Lord of heaven and earth, that you hid these things from the wise and understanding, and revealed them to infants.'" Matthew 11:25

Good morning!

Where I live, we often hear phrases like "What do you know?" as a casual greeting. It may seem like a simple question, but if we ponder its deeper meaning, we realize that what we think we know and the ultimate truth may not always be aligned. Our limited understanding can cloud our perception of reality.

During Jesus's time, the Pharisees were regarded as experts in the law and the knowledge of the Messiah. Yet, many of them failed to recognize Jesus as the Son of God because He didn't fit their preconceived notions. They were so focused on their own interpretations that they missed the truth standing right in front of them.

Similarly, we can easily be deceived by the facts we think we know while missing the bigger picture. Our understanding of the world is shaped by what we focus on and invest our thoughts into. While pursuing knowledge and seeking understanding is essential, we must humbly acknowledge our limitations.

Imagine embarking on a quest to learn about a fascinating subject, such as space. You read countless articles, watch documentaries, and absorb as much information as possible. Yet, no matter how much you learn, you realize that your knowledge remains only a glimpse of the vast mysteries of the universe. We are granted a portion of wisdom and understanding, but we can never fully grasp the magnitude of God's creation.

Today, let's take a moment to thank Him for the knowledge He reveals to us and also for the knowledge that He withholds from us. Let's pray that with each new discovery, we are reminded of His greatness and can appreciate His presence in every aspect of our lives.

Have a great day!

"Jesus took the loaves; and having given thanks, he distributed to the disciples, and the disciples to those who were sitting down; likewise also of the fish as much as they desired." John 6:11

Good morning!

Before feeding the multitude of 5000, Jesus noticed His exhausted disciples who hadn't even eaten due to their relentless service to the people. He led them to a quiet place for rest and nourishment. However, their plans were interrupted by a large crowd seeking Jesus' presence and teachings.

As the day went on, the disciples realized they were in a remote location and suggested sending the people away to find food and rest. To their surprise, Jesus challenged them, saying, "You give them something to eat." Given the crowd's size and limited resources, this seemed impossible to the disciples.

Despite feeling inadequate and lacking resources, Jesus asked the disciples to gather whatever food they could find. They came across a young boy with five loaves of bread and two fish—a seemingly insignificant amount. Yet, Jesus took this small offering, expressed gratitude, and multiplied it miraculously.

With the multiplied loaves and fish, Jesus fed the entire multitude abundantly. There were even twelve baskets of leftovers. This miracle highlights the power of gratitude in transforming scarcity into abundance, fear into faith, and doubt into assurance.

Similarly, in our lives, cultivating gratitude helps us recognize blessings, no matter how small or insignificant they may seem. When we give thanks for what we have, our perspective shifts from lack to sufficiency. Gratitude allows us to see miracles and blessings amidst challenges. All we need to do is open our eyes.

Have a great day!

"Enter into his gates with thanksgiving, into his courts with praise. Give thanks to him, and bless his name." Psalms 100:4

Good morning!

Growing up, I used to overlook the significance of singing in church. It seemed like just another routine, and I didn't fully grasp its purpose. As a shy child, I felt uneasy about singing in front of others, so I would quietly follow along or hum along to the music. Singing, to me, was an unfamiliar concept that people seemed to enjoy in church.

However, as I began to pay attention to what the Bible teaches, I discovered that singing is a form of worship and prayer. It is not merely a peculiar activity we engage in during church services. We are actually called to lift our voices in joyful praise and create music to honor our magnificent God.

Music has the power to convey our deepest emotions and carry a profound message. When we sing alone, our hearts can communicate a heartfelt expression to God. And when we sing in harmony with others, we can connect with fellow believers from different backgrounds and unite in praising God as one family.

Whether you sing, play an instrument, or hum along with others, let's enter into His presence with beautiful melodies of gratitude and praise. Please don't dismiss the songs as mere background noise; they hold a meaningful message waiting to be embraced.

Have a great day!

"Not that I speak because of lack, for I have learned in whatever state I am, to be content in it." Philippians 4:11

Good morning!

No matter the circumstances we find ourselves in, there is always room for improvement, and yet, things could also be much worse, couldn't they? By learning to embrace each day with a heart filled with gratitude for the blessings we currently have, we can discover happiness or, at the very least, inner peace in any situation. However, like all worthwhile endeavors, cultivating a habit of gratefulness requires conscious effort.

Yesterday, as I was returning home from running errands, my vehicle blew a tire. Under normal circumstances, this situation would have caused me great stress. The weather was sweltering, the absence of air-conditioning was uncomfortable, the mosquitoes were relentless, rain clouds loomed overhead, and I had plans for the evening. Moreover,

I didn't have a spare tire. However, thanks to my recent practice of gratitude, as I pulled over to the side of the road, a profound sense of gratefulness washed over me. I was grateful that no one was injured and it was just a tire. I appreciated my children's understanding of the situation, despite their hunger and eagerness to return home. I was grateful that it was still daylight and that my husband was only a couple of hours away and that he could come to our aid. I was relieved that the weather remained calm. Although our day took an unexpected turn, by actively seeking reasons to be grateful, my children and I remained content with our circumstances. In fact, we even found joy in our shared time together.

Let's practice the art of seeking and discovering countless reasons for gratitude. Instead of focusing on what we lack, let's acknowledge the abundance of blessings that surround us. By developing a daily habit of thanksgiving and praise, we can make it a natural and instinctive response to any and all of life's challenges.

Have a great day!

Generosity Unleashed

THE TRANSFORMATIVE POWER OF GENEROSITY IN GOD'S KINGDOM

"God said, 'Behold, I have given you every herb yielding seed, which is on the surface of all the earth, and every tree, which bears fruit yielding seed. It will be your food.'" Genesis 1:29

Good morning!

As we begin our exploration of generosity, let's first acknowledge the ultimate source of all generosity, God. From the very beginning, God created the heavens, the earth, and everything in between, including us. He lovingly formed us and gave us the gift of life, providing an abundance of food to nourish our bodies, companionship so that we are not alone, and dominion over all of the earth.

But God's generosity did not stop there. Even though we are rebellious and sinful, He continues to shower us with blessings. Despite our flaws, He chooses to love us, and out of His grace and mercy, He provides everything we need to flourish. God seeks goodness for all of His creation, and He is full of compassion and generosity.

As we grow in our understanding and experience of God's generosity toward us, let's also grow in our generosity toward others. May our hearts be open to giving freely and cheerfully, just as God has given to us.

Have a great day!

"For the wages of sin is death, but the free gift of God is eternal life in Christ Jesus our Lord."
Romans 6:23

Good morning!

As I read this verse, I can't help but be moved by God's sacrificial love. He willingly gave His only Son so that we could be saved from the consequences of our sins.

Jesus' purpose on earth extended far beyond personal pleasure or gain. His mission was rooted in compassion and selflessness. He came to teach us how to live, to ignite faith within us, and ultimately, to offer His life so that we may have eternal life.

Throughout His earthly journey, Jesus demonstrated more than sacrificial love. He dedicated His time and energy to serving others, imparting wisdom on how to live lives filled with love and forgiveness. Patiently, He answered our questions, providing evidence of His existence.

Jesus held nothing back; He gave every part of Himself, desiring only our love in return.

Through Jesus, we are offered a pathway to experience joy in this world, and with faith in Him, we are also given the opportunity to live happily ever after. God's love knows no bounds; it overflows with generosity. Isn't He truly wonderful?

Today, let's not only remember God's love and sacrifice but also embrace the gifts He freely gives us. Let's strive to live a life that reflects His sacrificial love and points others toward the abundant life found in Jesus.

Have a great day!

"But a certain Samaritan, as he traveled, came where he was. When he saw him, he was moved with compassion, came to him, and bound up his wounds, pouring on oil and wine. He set him on his own animal, brought him to an inn, and took care of him." Luke 10:33-34

Good morning!

In this touching parable, Jesus tells of a traveler who fell victim to robbers, left wounded and helpless on the roadside. While many passed by without concern, it was a Samaritan who saw him and was filled with compassion. Without hesitation, he went above and beyond to aid the wounded stranger. He tended to his wounds, provided transportation, and ensured his ongoing care at an inn.

Jesus shared this story to teach us about the true meaning of being a neighbor and how we should treat one another. The Samaritan recognized someone in desperate need and took immediate action.

How often have we encountered people in distress and felt a sense of empathy yet hesitated to assist? Our reservations may stem from concerns about personal safety, fear of exploitation, or the belief that we lack the time or resources to make a difference. However, we are called to be moved by compassion when we encounter those in need, even if it inconveniences us.

As we journey through today, let's be attentive to those around us, refusing to turn a blind eye. Instead, let's extend a helping hand in any way we can. This is how we demonstrate love for our neighbors. If a situation seems unsafe or beyond our capabilities, we can still offer support by calling a professional for help and fervently praying for their well-being. Let's be intentional in noticing the people who cross our paths and be a source of comfort.

Have a great day!

"Honor Yahweh with your substance, with the first fruits of all your increase; so your barns will be filled with plenty, and your vats will overflow with new wine." Proverbs 3:9-10

Good morning!

I have come to realize that true generosity requires a shift in perspective. I used to believe that giving to others was something I could only do if I had more than enough income or an abundance of time. However, this limited mindset contradicts the true essence of giving as taught in the Bible.

In Proverbs, we are encouraged to honor God by offering Him the first fruits of our harvest and blessings. It's a call to prioritize generosity, offering our best, and giving cheerfully. It's not about giving others what's left over but about placing God and others at the forefront of our hearts and actions.

As I reflect on this verse, I can no longer make excuses about not having enough resources or time to help others. Instead, I am called to step out in faith and prioritize the needs of others, and by doing so, I affirm my faith in God's provision over my life. As Jesus said, "Give, and it will be given to you: good measure, pressed down, shaken together, and running over, will be given to you. For with the same measure you measure it will be measured back to you" (Luke 6:38).

Today, let's make a conscious effort to honor God and pursue a spirit of generosity by prioritizing the needs of others and giving wholeheartedly. True generosity isn't about the size of our gifts; it's about the love and care we put into it. Our acts of kindness, no matter how small they may seem, can bring hope and joy to those in need.

Have a great day!

"But who am I, and what is my people, that we should be able to offer so willingly as this? For all things come from you, and we have given you of your own." 1 Chronicles 29:14

Good morning!

In this verse, King David humbly acknowledges the generosity of the people who willingly contributed resources to build the temple of God. As he ponders their heartfelt offerings, he recognizes the true source of their abundance. David's words resonate with humility and gratitude, acknowledging that everything they gave ultimately came from God. He states, "We have given you of your own," understanding that their contributions were merely a return of the blessings bestowed upon them.

David's perspective challenges us to examine our own hearts and how we utilize the resources God has entrusted to us. Do we approach our possessions with a sense of entitlement and self-centeredness, or do we recognize that everything we have is a gift from God? Let us learn from David's example and strive to be good stewards of the blessings in our lives, using them to honor God and advance His kingdom.

As we reflect upon the abundance we enjoy, may we adopt an attitude of gratitude and a desire to align our actions with God's purposes. Let us prayerfully consider how we can use our resources, time, talents, and material possessions to bring glory to God and bless others.

Today, let's remember that all things come from God, and in response, let us give generously, love extravagantly, and live faithfully as stewards of His abundant blessings.

Have a great day!

"He said, 'This is what I will do. I will pull down my barns, build bigger ones, and there I will store all my grain and my goods. I will tell my soul, "Soul, you have many goods laid up for many years. Take your ease, eat, drink, and be merry."'" Luke 12:18-19

Good morning!

In this parable, Jesus tells the story of a rich man who plans to store up his abundance, thinking that he can secure a worry-free future for himself. Jesus refers to him as a fool, highlighting the faults of this kind of mindset. Jesus reminds us that life is about more than material possessions, and our true value extends beyond what we consume and accumulate.

The image of storing up goods in a barn reminds me of a squirrel collecting seeds. Have you ever seen a squirrel at a bird feeder? It's pretty comical to watch. The squirrel gets so excited and tries to collect from it, protect it, and claim the feeder for itself, unaware that it will be refilled again the next day.

Like the squirrel hoarding seeds, we may be tempted to accumulate resources for ourselves. However, Jesus invites us to adopt a different perspective. He calls us to have faith and to recognize that true abundance is found in Him. Rather than obsessively accumulating and guarding our possessions, Jesus invites us to share with others.

Today, Instead of worrying about the future, let's trust God's faithfulness and use our resources to bless others. We can reflect on our attitudes toward material possessions and consider how to be more generous with what we have been given.

Have a great day!

"For judgment is without mercy to him who has shown no mercy. Mercy triumphs over judgment."
James 2:13

Good morning!

Generosity goes beyond the act of giving material resources; it also includes spreading kindness and compassion. It's easy to be kind when others are kind to us, but true generosity shines when we extend kindness to those who may not deserve it.

In our daily interactions, it's inevitable that we may encounter people who hurt us, whether intentionally or unintentionally. The words and actions we choose in response can either perpetuate the cycle of hurt or break it with love and generosity. When faced with rudeness from a neighbor, coworker, family member, or even a stranger, how do we choose to respond?

Instead of hastily labeling someone as rude, we can choose to rise above that kind of negativity and respond with kindness. While it may be challenging, sowing seeds of kindness—offering a genuine compliment, performing a small favor, or simply being polite—can nurture relationships and create a positive ripple effect. Your response might just be the start of a better day for them, and they, in turn, might extend kindness to others.

Today, let's sow seeds of kindness regardless of the circumstances we find ourselves in. No matter what kind of fertilizer we are working with, whether it's rudeness, criticism, or challenging situations, we can respond with love, understanding, and generosity. By doing so, we can reflect on how mercy triumphs over judgment, allowing our relationships to flourish and making a positive impact on the lives of those around us.

Have a great day!

"His Lord said to him, 'Well done, good and faithful servant. You have been faithful over a few things. I will set you over many things. Enter into the joy of your Lord.'" Matthew 25:23

Good morning!

Have you ever stopped to consider the gifts and blessings you've received? In the parable shared by Jesus, we learn about the faithful servants who wisely invested the resources entrusted to them by their master. They were able to double their master's money, and their faithfulness was rewarded.

However, there was one servant who was afraid and buried his portion, failing to make good use of what he had been given. The master was disappointed with this servant's lack of initiative.

This parable holds a powerful lesson for us. Jesus is calling us to use the gifts, time, skills, and resources that He has blessed us with to make a positive impact on His kingdom. Each of us has unique abilities and resources at our disposal, and it is our responsibility to use them wisely and generously.

Consider how you can invest your blessings in ways that honor God and bless others. It could be supporting clean water initiatives, donating Bibles to those who haven't heard the Good News, supporting your local church, or simply extending a helping hand to someone in need. No act of kindness or investment is too small when done with a heart that desires to serve God and others.

Remember, we may have different amounts of resources, but we all share the same call to steward them faithfully. I want to encourage you to take time to read this parable in your Bible and reflect on how you can use your unique gifts and resources to bless others. Let's embrace the responsibility of being faithful stewards and invest our gifts and resources in ways that honor God.

Have a great day!

"Each of you not just looking to his own things, but each of you also to the things of others."
Philippians 2:4

Good Morning!

In today's fast-paced world, time is often seen as a scarce commodity. We constantly rush from one task to another, preoccupied with our own agendas. But what if we took a moment to consider the power of being generous with our time?

This is something I've come to cherish deeply. As a busy parent, I find myself caught up in a never-ending cycle of responsibilities, always planning, cleaning, cooking, working, and so much more. Although my children often ask me to play with them, I am too busy or too tired to participate in any of their activities. In the midst of it all, I recently realized that I rarely make time for others.

Imagine the impact we could make if we consciously offered our time and attention to those around us. There are people in our lives who often go unnoticed, longing for someone to care, to listen, or to simply be present. Is there someone in your life who could benefit from your help, your listening ear, or a friendly visit? It could be a family member, a friend, a colleague, or even a stranger in need.

Let's make an intentional effort to set aside distractions and offer our undivided time and attention. We can start at home, within our families, and extend it to others we encounter throughout the day. Remember, time is a precious gift, and when we spend it on others, it'll prove to be a worthwhile investment.

Have a great day!

"that they do good, that they be rich in good works, that they be ready to distribute, willing to share;"
1 Timothy 6:18

Good morning!

In Paul's letter to Timothy, we learn that, as Christians, it is essential to actively participate in our communities and look for ways to serve and uplift others. Paul's words inspire us to lead a life of service and selflessness, always ready to extend a helping hand to anyone who needs it, whether they are family, friends, or strangers.

As followers of Christ, we are called to live a life of outrageous generosity, reflecting His love and compassion. Our actions should be a reflection of our faith, and we should strive to be known for our kindness and generosity. By our words and deeds, we can make a positive impact on the world around us.

Therefore, let's take these words to heart and be motivated by love to be generous with our time and resources. Let's think of ways to make a difference in the lives of those around us. We can use our unique talents and skills to bless others, whether it's through volunteering, helping a neighbor in need, or simply offering ideas and advice. Let's be creative in our approach and help lift others up.

Have a great day!

"Let each man give according as he has determined in his heart, not grudgingly or under compulsion, for God loves a cheerful giver." 2 Corinthians 9:7

Good morning!

I believe that giving can be a truly fulfilling and joyful experience. When the opportunity arises to give a gift, I like to create homemade crafts and put together gift baskets for others. I get so excited to personalize and include unique items for people that it's such a delightful experience.

Yet, I must admit, I'm not a fan of watching someone open my gifts. I often feel anxious and wonder if the recipient will like it or not. While I may be a little shy or uneasy about giving gifts, I still enjoy doing it. My hope is that when they open my gift, they can get a sense of the depth of love and care I have for them through the time, effort, and thoughtfulness that went into making it.

However, there are moments when giving feels less appealing. Maybe it's when faced with taxes, contributing to charities that might not appreciate it, or giving money to those who may misuse it. In such situations, it's crucial to remember that giving should never be driven by obligation or guilt. Instead, it should always be a voluntary act of love carried out with a cheerful heart.

So, how should we respond when we find ourselves reluctant to give? The best course of action is to turn to prayer and seek guidance from the Lord. We can ask Him to help us overcome any prideful thoughts and gain clarity on how to responsibly utilize His resources so that our giving will truly bless those who receive it.

Today, as you go about your day, I encourage you to consider the joy of giving. Remember that giving isn't merely an obligation; it is a privilege. It is an expression of God's love working through us. So, let's give willingly, cheerfully, and with open hearts.

Have a great day!

"Jesus said to him, 'If you want to be perfect, go, sell what you have, and give to the poor, and you will have treasure in heaven; and come, follow me.'"
Matthew 19:21

Good morning!

In this passage from the Bible, a young man approached Jesus, believing he had followed all the commandments. He asked Jesus what more he could do to attain perfection. Jesus responded by telling him to sell his possessions, give to the poor, and follow Him. This instruction made the young man sad because he had many possessions.

This encounter challenges us to examine our own hearts and consider what we may be holding onto that is preventing us from giving generously. It's easy to become caught up in the pursuit of material wealth and possessions, but Jesus teaches us that we should be generous and give to those in need. When we do so, we not only bless others but also receive eternal rewards.

While not everyone may be called to sell everything they own, we can all embrace the spirit of generosity and sacrificial giving. For example, we can take the time to assess our belongings and donate items we no longer need. We can also set aside a percentage of our income and dedicate it to charities and helping others. By trusting in the Giver of all blessings and following Him, we can live a fulfilling and generous life by seeking ways to bless others.

Have a great day!

"'Give, and it will be given to you: good measure, pressed down, shaken together, and running over, will be given to you. For with the same measure you measure it will be measured back to you.'" Luke 6:38

Good morning!

I love how Jesus encourages us to give generously and exceed expectations. When I was growing up, I worked at a bait store where we had an abundance of minnows. This abundance mindset allowed us to be generous and serve our customers with joy.

We didn't need to count the minnows or worry about running low. In fact, we would often give customers two or three times the amount of minnows they asked for. Giving a heaping scoop was always a pleasure for me because I got to see their surprise and gratitude.

Similarly, God's blessings toward us are abundant and overflowing. He gives us more than enough and wants us to share our blessings with others. We should not hold back, give sparingly, or keep track of our generous gifts. Instead, we should seek to give abundantly with a sincere desire to help others and honor God. The joy of giving is a gift in itself.

I pray that we will continue to grow in our desire to give unconditionally, in good measure, and from the heart. Today, Let's embrace the abundance mindset and smile as we serve others a heaping scoop.

Have a great day!

"He called his disciples to himself and said to them, 'Most certainly I tell you, this poor widow gave more than all those who are giving into the treasury, for they all gave out of their abundance, but she, out of her poverty, gave all that she had to live on.'" Mark 12:43-44

Good morning!

In this passage, Jesus gathers His disciples and shares a profound lesson with them. He highlights the sacrificial giving of a poor widow whose humble offering surpassed the gifts of those who gave out of their surplus. Despite her limited resources, she poured out everything she had, an act of wholehearted devotion.

This widow's remarkable example challenges us to consider the motivation behind our own giving. Are we simply offering from our abundance, giving what is convenient and comfortable? Or are we willing to step beyond our limitations and give sacrificially, pouring out our hearts and resources with love and faith?

As we conclude this journey together, let's reflect and draw inspiration from the widow's unwavering commitment. May her story remind us that the impact of our offerings is not measured by their size or quantity but by the depth of love and sacrifice they represent.

Just as the widow's small yet meaningful gift echoed through time, our acts of kindness, compassion, and generosity have the power to leave a lasting imprint on the lives we touch. So, let's continue to embrace each day, guided by God's love and grace, being open to change and ready to make a difference to bring glory to His name.

As you go on the next chapter of your spiritual journey, I pray that God will bless you abundantly and that you will continually seek His guidance in every step you take.

Have a great day!

Resources

Benner, J. A. (1999). Hebrew Word Definition: Sin. Ancient Hebrew Research Center. Retrieved July 20, 2020, from https://www.ancient-hebrew.org/definition/sin.htm

[Bible Project]. (2018, March 18). Word Studies Khata / Sin [Video]. BibleProject. https://bibleproject.com/explore/video/khata-sin/

Forerunner Commentary (1992). What the Bible says about Sin as missing the mark. Bible Tools. Retrieved July 20, 2020, from https://www.bibletools.org/index.cfm/fuseaction

/topical.show/RTD/cgg/ID/6773/Sin-as-Missing
-Mark.htm

Life.Church (2008). World English Bible WEBUS.
YouVersion [Mobile app].
https://www.youversion.com/the-bible-app/(Ori
ginal work published 1999)

Thank You!

Dear Reader,

As we approach the conclusion of this transformative journey together, I want to express my deepest gratitude for joining me on this path of embracing each day with God's Word. Your commitment and dedication have been truly inspiring, and I hope this book has brought you closer to Him and enriched your life in unimaginable ways, as it did for me.

Now, I would like to make a special request. Reviews play a significant role in helping others discover meaningful resources that can positively impact their lives. Please consider leaving a review for this book and sharing your thoughts and experiences with others. Your review can guide others on their journeys of growth and spiritual enrichment.

I aim to reach 100 reviews for this book, and your contribution can make a tremendous difference in achieving this milestone. Your honest feedback is precious, regardless of whether your journey was filled with triumphs, challenges, or a mix of both. Your review will be an authentic testament to this book's impact on your life and provide valuable insights for potential readers.

Once again, I express my heartfelt appreciation for your presence on this journey. Your support and participation have been invaluable, and I am genuinely grateful to have had the opportunity to share this experience with you. May we continue to embrace each day with God's Word as our guide, nurturing our spirits and fostering a life of purpose and fulfillment.

With love,

Amy

Made in the USA
Monee, IL
11 June 2024

59239708R00118